Examining Levels of Involvement in the Early Years

Examining Levels of Involvement in the Early Years studies the theory and rationale behind using young children's levels of involvement as a tool for enhancing their experiential learning in diverse settings by exploring values, beliefs, ideology, resourcefulness and environmental contexts.

Drawing on Laevers' process-oriented Self-evaluation Instrument for Care Settings and the Leuven Involvement Scale for Young Children, this book examines the theoretical constructs that underpin the development of these instruments as well as the practical implications of how and why practitioners may use the scales in their settings. More importantly, it looks at children's deep level learning capabilities and reflects on the engaging possibilities this presents.

Using encounters with children and adults from a range of settings, it covers:

- connecting levels of involvement with local, national, international and theoretical approaches;
- embracing levels of involvement;
- involving the environment;
- levels of outdoor involvement;
- engaging with adult involvement;
- nurturing involvement through observation, assessment and planning.

Including contributions from experts in the field, this book will be essential reading for students, trainee early years practitioners and all those wanting to continue their professional learning.

Annie Woods is a former early years lecturer, programme leader and academic team leader in the education department at Nottingham Trent University, UK. Trained as a forest school leader and a former assistant head teacher, she has also edited two further books: *Child-initiated Play and Learning* and *The Characteristics of Effective Learning*, both for Routledge.

Examining Levels of Involvement in the Early Years

Engaging with children's possibilities

Edited by Annie Woods

Routledge
Taylor & Francis Group

LONDON AND NEW YORK

First published 2016
by Routledge
2 Park Square, Milton Park, Abingdon, Oxon OX14 4RN

and by Routledge
711 Third Avenue, New York, NY 10017

Routledge is an imprint of the Taylor & Francis Group, an informa business

© 2016 selection and editorial matter, Annie Woods; individual chapters, the contributors

The right of Annie Woods to be identified as the author of the editorial material, and of the authors for their individual chapters, has been asserted in accordance with sections 77 and 78 of the Copyright, Designs and Patents Act 1988.

British Library Cataloguing in Publication Data
A catalogue record for this book is available from the British Library

Library of Congress Cataloging in Publication Data
Names: Woods, Annie, editor.
Title: Examining levels of involvement in the early years : engaging with children's possibilities / edited by Annie Woods.
Description: New York, NY : Routledge, 2016.
Identifiers: LCCN 2015030802| ISBN 9781138885004 (hbk) |
ISBN 9781138885011 (pbk) | ISBN 9781315715735 (ebk)
Subjects: LCSH: Experiential learning. | Early childhood education.
Classification: LCC LB1027.23 .E95 2016 | DDC 372.21—dc23
LC record available at http://lccn.loc.gov/2015030802

ISBN: 978-1-138-88500-4 (hbk)
ISBN: 978-1-138-88501-1 (pbk)
ISBN: 978-1-315-71573-5 (ebk)

Typeset in Bembo
by Book Now Ltd, London

Printed in Great Britain by Ashford Colour Press Ltd., Gosport, Hampshire.

Contents

Contributors

Editor

Annie Woods has recently retired from Nottingham Trent University where she held a number of roles as an early years lecturer, programme leader and academic team leader in the education department. She has developed a number of programmes and routes to early years qualifications and has been an external examiner in three universities. Prior to working in higher education, Annie taught in foundation stage and had been an assistant head teacher. Trained as a forest school leader, she has also edited two further books: *Child-initiated Play and Learning* and *The Characteristics of Effective Learning* for Routledge.

Contributors

Victoria Brown is a principal lecturer at Nottingham Trent University where she has been an early years lecturer and course leader for primary education. Prior to working in higher education, Victoria worked for a local authority as a foundation stage advisory teacher attached to a children's centre and as a primary and early years teacher for many years. A trained forest school leader, she has a particular interest in learning in nature and recently visited Scandinavian countries to learn more about this approach.

Catherine Gripton was a teacher in Nottingham and Nottinghamshire primary schools for 14 years, teaching children across the 3–7 age range and becoming an advanced skills teacher. She is currently a senior lecturer in primary and early years initial teacher education at Nottingham Trent University.

Julie Kent is a lecturer and joint course leader on the Childhood Studies BA course at Nottingham Trent University. Prior to working in higher education, she led the team in a Sure Start children's centre in Northamptonshire with a focus on developing both inter-agency working and early communication support for children and families. She is also a qualified speech and language therapist, trainer for the Early Language Development Programme and is a Makaton regional tutor.

Vicky McEwan is a trained forest school leader and started her career as a nursery nurse before training to become a teacher and school governor. She also owned and managed a day nursery before moving into early years advisory work. She currently lectures on early years programmes at Nottingham Trent University where she supports trainee teachers in schools.

Sally McMeeking gained an NNEB qualification and worked as a nanny before becoming a teaching assistant in a small school with an interest in special educational needs, specifically behavioural problems. She gained her degree in Early Childhood Education and is currently an early years professional in a privately owned nursery leading practice and mentoring staff.

Moira Moran taught and led teams in nursery units and schools for more than 20 years, first in London then in Nottingham. She subsequently joined a team of local authority early years specialist teachers supporting the PVI sector and teachers in Foundation Units. A trained forest school trainer, she currently leads the Childhood Studies course in addition to lecturing on the Early Years Initial Teacher Training pathways. Her research area is early play.

Danusia Taylor has worked in childcare for 11 years. She began as a volunteer and became an employee after completing her childcare qualifications as a practitioner. Once qualified, she took over the running of the nursery and became an Early Years Professional in 2012. She is currently studying for an MA.

Acknowledgements

Many husbands, partners and practitioners have supported our deep levels of involvement in playing with children, learning with adults and writing with each other. Thank you for containing our enjoyment and aspirations – you know who you are: Bright Sparks preschool, Steve, Felicity, Dean, David, Juliet, Fran, Sarah, Sue, Di, Kirsty, Suzanne, Veronica, Andy, Gerard and Lemming.

Introduction

Annie Woods

The desire for children to be deeply involved in their own activities has permeated our first two books (*Child-initiated Play and Learning: Planning for Possibilities in the Early Years*, 2013 and *The Characteristics of Effective Learning: Creating and Capturing the Possibilities in the Early Years*, 2014) through exploring adults' planning for possibilities; empathic observation following children's interests; leaderful settings; and embracing dispositional characteristics of effective learning. This approach and philosophy has been based on many years' practice and, we suggest, transcends the frequently changing, early years curriculum landscape over the last 30 years or so. Our writing and teaching has embraced the term 'levels of involvement' and as readers, we anticipate that you are familiar with the term too. Many of you will have attended training provided by local authorities and early years associations, participated in the Effective Early Learning project (EEL; Pascal and Bertram, 1997) and the more recent Baby Effective Early Learning project (BEEL; Pascal and Bertram, 2005), and attended research and training events and national conferences where Ferre Laevers has presented his research begun in 1976. Laevers continues this research with others, and both introduces and illustrates his continued research with videos of children and the Leuven Involvement Scale for Young Children (LIS-YC; Laevers, 1994), developed at the Centre of Experiential Education, Leuven, Belgium, and disseminated throughout the United Kingdom and across Europe, Australia and New Zealand over the last 25 years.

This book considers the thinking behind looking at young children's levels of involvement as a tool for enhancing their experiential learning in our settings by scrutinising values, beliefs, ideology, planning, resourcefulness and environmental contexts. Drawing on Ferre Laevers' research, the authors examine the theoretical constructs that appear to have influenced experiential education (EXE); how the process of measuring well-being and involvement is and can be used in settings; the impact using the scales and observation methodology has had on every-day early years practice; children's deeper level learning; and adult involvement. We look at children's deep level learning capabilities and reflect on the engaging possibilities this presents. We use encounters from a range of settings and demonstrate how and why practitioners may use the LIS-YC in their settings and offer provocative questions to afford opportunities for students and practitioners to reflect and self-evaluate. This provides a rich potential for our own continued learning as professionals. Primarily, becoming aware of children's levels of involvement, and then agreeing a score are only part of the process; it is what we do with that information that is crucial.

We acknowledge that our exploration is one of interpretation and subjectivity. Laevers refers to the theorists we consider in this book, but not in substantive detail.

His published papers, research and conference presentations repeatedly affirm Piaget, Rogers and Csíkszentmihályi as influential. We also infer the ideas of Rogoff, Bronfenbrenner, Vygotsky, Dewey and Isaacs. Laevers (2009) also considers the approaches of High Scope, Reggio Emilia and Te Whāriki as having a similar 'open framework approach', focusing on learning, dispositions, children's interests and projects, rather than a fixed curriculum with specific outcomes and targets.

> The core element for experiential education is that you take the experience of the other, of the learner, as a point of reference in whatever you do. So meaning that you try to sense, to feel, to understand how others make sense of the world.
>
> (Laevers, 2009: online)

There is an echo of Froebel, Rousseau and Steiner in 'if what you do is leading to wellbeing in children and higher levels of involvement' (ibid.): the child at the centre of the education process. I distinctly recall the first time I watched the training video and read the manual from 1997 (Laevers *et al.*, 1997) where Moon and Laevers introduce experiential education (EXE). The class of young children have been offered fresh rhubarb to look at, eat, cook and explore. One child experimented with pepper, one with sugar – but it is the child who finds the spider deep down in the rhubarb leaf who then becomes deeply involved in researching spiders, with Moon, as teacher, facilitating the spontaneous learning journey. The planning was for possibilities with rhubarb, outcomes unknown but evidently rich for learning potential, observed and documented in the moment as the child, as Vygotsky (1978: 102) states, 'in play it as though he were a head taller than himself'. Moon (1997: 12) herself commented: 'Preparing the things on offer makes me feel ready for the day. The real adventure can then take off. Because nobody knows how it will turn out.'

> Accidentally the children discover a spider. This incident is not seen as a disturbance of the activity that was going on, i.e. cutting and tasting rhubarb. On the contrary, the teacher adopts a flexible attitude and welcomes the spider as an opportunity to exploit the children's exploratory drive. Again, an open form of organisation is essential for this. We notice how the children [also] learn to be flexible and unexpected events within an open organisation form and how they begin to guide themselves. … The teacher helps the children get several new experiences out of the incident with the spider. She explicitly demands the children's attention and encourages them to observe carefully and to describe what they see. She also invites them to let the spider walk over their finger or leg and feel this new sensation for themselves. … The teacher introduces a book on insects […] and they learn to relate symbols, signs and pictures to the reality they are involved in at a specific moment.
>
> (Laevers *et al.*, 1997: 42–43)

As Rinaldi (in Dahlberg and Moss, 2005: 106–107) has observed:

> Learning does not proceed in a linear way, determined and deterministic, by progressive and predictable stages, but rather is constructed through contemporaneous advances, standstills and 'retreats' that take many directions … it is sensitive to the rhythms of communication and incorporates the significance of timing and children's

investigations and research. … The teacher and child become partners in a process of experimentation and research, in which the children invent a problem before they search for solutions.

Rogoff (1990: 193) has told us that 'in investigations of learning to plan, research suggests that school-age children profit from guided participation with partners who are skilled in planning'. This research underpins Laevers (2005: 8), who tells us that

> well-being and involvement are welcomed by teachers as most stimulating and helpful in improving the quality of their work. The concepts of wellbeing and involvement *match the intuitions* [my italics] of many teachers and give them a scientifically-based confirmation of what they knew already: when we can get children into that 'flow state', development must and will take place within the area(s) addressed by the activity.

We anticipate that you are familiar with the concept of levels of involvement and the ideas and practice within this book and feel as if you *know* what we explore here, intuitively. Much of what Laevers has said and written is deceptive in its simplicity, and thus commands our highest respect and regard. It has led to the development and widespread use of the LIS-YC.

> That is what Experiential Education is about: exploiting and enhancing the energy in people and drawing them into a positive spiral which engenders deep level learning. Only in this way can we make schools more effective and strong enough to meet the challenges of education: the development of adults who are self-confident and mentally healthy, curious and exploratory, expressive and communicative, imaginative and creative, full of initiative, well-organised …
>
> (Laevers, 2005: 9)

Dubiel (2015) cites the *Guardian* (December, 2014) and the current education minister:

> Spelling out her personal priorities, Morgan says she wants to focus on 'character education'. 'What I mean is a focus on things like the additional character skills we all need to get on in life – resilience, grit, self-esteem, self-confidence.'

In 2014, Ofsted highlighted outstanding practice:

> Children are highly motivated, very eager to join in and consistently demonstrate characteristics of effective learning with high levels of curiosity, imagination and concentration. They listen intently and are highly responsive to adults and each other. They do not distract others or become distracted themselves.

We would argue that this is achieved by children demonstrating high levels of involvement within nurturing, stimulating environments, who are afforded the time, space and opportunities to experience, experiment and engage in deeply satisfying activities.

The tool developed in the Leuven Institute is a Process-Oriented Self-evaluation Monitoring System (POMS) and focuses strongly on the importance of the process and quality of learning. Many local authorities have encouraged their settings to incorporate the involvement and well-being scales as an 'agreed and consistent methodology' where 'we can measure processes and achievements in learning in other ways rather than looking at outcomes' (Wiltshire County Council: online). In 2015, Laevers reported on research with Kent County Council and Milton Keynes on 'Wellbeing and involvement: The shortcut to sustainable development for every child' (Nursery World Show and Conference, February, 2015). There has been a strong relationship between Laevers and local authorities in the United Kingdom over the last ten years but, in the current climate, we have a *feeling,* however, that further quality measures are being inferred by local authorities; for example, whether the *number* of level 4 or 5 involved children (Leuven Scales) is used as an outcome rather than a process measure alongside ECERS (the Early Childhood Environment Rating Scale), ITERS (the Infant Toddler Environment Rating Scale) and baseline assessment. Laevers (2007: 55) comments:

> One of the most dramatic implications of the concept of 'deep level learning' has to be situated in the field of educational *evaluation.* What we have to question is not so much the eagerness (especially by education authorities) to measure the outcome of schools.

At the Nursery World conference and master class in February 2015, Laevers talked of the UK insistence on *explicit* outcomes for measuring quality. He was equally insistent that *quality is at the level of process* amongst early years practitioners. This continues to be a past, present and future debate, and he said 'professionals can make judgements, not technicians with a recipe'. Dubiel, at the same conference, explored the difficulties faced by practitioners with the onset of non-statutory baseline assessment proposed for 2016 with the six models available to use. Only one model uses direct observation, including levels of well-being and involvement; the other five use models of testing and he asks to what extent significant learning can be assessed when reduced to a generated score.

This book aims to continue previous discussions on planning for possibilities, and children's characteristics of effective learning with high levels of involvement described in authentic encounters with children. Like Laevers (Nursery World Show and Conference, 2015: my conference notes), 'the focus on process, feedback given immediately, so next zone of proximal development occurs changing the feel of the child, will empower parents, they begin to have hope.' He states:

> *Involvement is on its own the reflection of intense mental life. Involvement is not limited to one type of activity. Involvement is at the junction of a wide variety of forces. Involvement does include social interaction. Involvement [welcomes] the teacher's intuitions.* Let's start where we are and acknowledge what you have built up until now. Whatever the level of involvement is at this moment, let's join our efforts, as a team, to have that level raised. In this perspective, even a small improvement as a result of a deliberately taken initiative, is experienced as a success, from which new energy is gained

to make another step. Using involvement does not pin the teachers down. It gives them the means to feel rewarded!

(Laevers, 2002: 19)

We contend, therefore, that high levels of involvement signal highly relevant and appropriateness of environmental spaces, activities on offer and engagement of staff, who themselves feel a deep satisfaction and level of well-being.

In Chapter 1, I explore Laevers' research and writings to discover the many theoretical influences that underpin his approach to experiential education and how the Leuven Involvement Scale for Young Children (LIS-YC) was developed to support practitioner evaluation of both the environment and the level of involvement and well-being of children within that environment. The theoretical framework reflects ideas from John Dewey, Jean Piaget, Lev Vygotsky, Carl Rogers and Mihalyi Csíkszentmihályi in particular, and Laevers frequently refers to their influence in his many journal articles and conference presentations. A synopsis of these ideas is offered to remind us of the philosophical mosaic at the foundation of effective early years practice. The inference, therefore, is one of child centredness, experiential learning, social constructivism and an exploration of how one acts and can be seen to be acting as a deeply engaged learner. For Laevers, a high level of involvement is a signal of deep level learning and one, that from as early as 1976, he has intended to be used as practitioner critical reflection on practice.

Having explored many of the theories that appear to have influenced the development of the practical instrument of LIS-YC, in Chapter 2 I write about a brief research activity with a landscape architect (www.landscapesnaturally.co.uk) and an early years setting. I explore, with others, how to use the instrument to look for signals of involvement in children and thus how to use what we see to evaluate provision. In this instance, an early years setting was beginning a process to relocate and hoped to use the findings to design a more appropriate and exciting outdoor space. Felicity Robinson, when offering feedback on the activity and discussion wrote:

> As a landscape architect I am fascinated about the way environment influences behaviour (in the widest sense) and I have done a lot of research into this over the years. The Laevers Involvement Scale is another 'way of seeing' for me that I shall certainly use in my observation of early years settings in the future as part of the design process. Many settings are cluttered with too much fixed equipment and/or are over 'designed' as we know, with few opportunities for children to be absorbed by natural materials and the 'affordances' offered by subtle design. I go so far as to think that all designers of environments for children should have some understanding of Laevers' work … and certainly there is potential for practitioners to collaborate with landscape designers in this way.
>
> (Felicity Robinson, 2014: personal
communication)

Laevers' process-oriented approach is empowering and enlightening, for practitioners working with children as well as adult learners, the outcomes emerging as the process evolves. Watching a volunteer's involvement with children enriched practitioner reflection at the end of the morning and provoked much discussion. The research presented here is explored by other authors in further chapters, a grounding of theoretical principles having been established in the first two chapters.

In Chapter 3, Victoria Brown explores Laevers' Ten Action Points (Laevers *et al.*, 1997). She has three aims and explores planning and provision for individual needs; the socio-cultural context and the content – what a child is offered; and the curriculum in its broadest sense within the learning environment. In a sense, the Ten Action Points elaborate both the theories underpinning Laevers' ideas and the Involvement Scales. The 'points of action' are the evaluative questions and areas to consider, having observed the children and the environment they are working within, in order to raise the quality of learning that may occur, raise the levels of involvement and well-being, and differentiate spaces and activities for individual children's interests to flourish. Victoria has worked closely with a teacher in this chapter, as well as drawing upon her long experience with trainee teachers.

'Learning as a community process' (Rogoff *et al.*, 2001) forms the content of Chapter 4, a collaboration between Moira Moran and two early years professionals (EYPs). The project sought to evaluate the impact of outdoor experiences on children's levels of involvement in forest school type activities. The chapter is dialogic, and as Malaguzzi might have described it, 'a game of ping-pong' where ideas (the ball) are batted across to each other for comment and reflection. It has been important for us as authors in this book, to both highlight the theoretical constructs underpinning 'levels of involvement' as well as offer authentic practice to illustrate how the process of watching children involved in deep level learning has become part of our everyday practice. As in our earlier books, encounters with children and adults illuminate and refresh our own understanding and will resonate with many early years practitioners.

Vicky McEwan has been involved with undertaking and leading EEL (1997) and BEEL (2005) practice and in Chapter 5 explores the crucial importance of adult engagement in children's involvement. She explores the Adult Style Observation System (ASOS, 1997), which Laevers *et al.* developed to further support critical reflection and evaluation of settings and practitioner skills and attitudes. Much of what Vicky discusses reflects Wenger's notion of 'community of practice' and is based on key leadership dispositions.

This is further explored in Chapter 6 by Julie Kent who documents a professional and personal journey of leading a children's centre, whose ethos of an inclusive and containing environment was further enhanced by adopting Laevers' approach to observing children and adults in settings. The journey, although based in one setting, will be a familiar one; staff striving to offer families and community a nurturing environment whilst trying to balance and incorporate ever-changing, external demands in a real exploration of Bronfenbrenner's Ecological System. As leader, Julie 'contained' staff training, morale and holistic philosophy, which is now benefitting emerging practitioners as they make a study of child development, family and community in context, and leadership theory.

Catherine Gripton, in the final chapter, links her ideas to our first two books. She encapsulates our philosophy of drawing upon shared experiences with children to make authentic and meaningful sense of what we see and then to nurture specific children's possibilities through our provision. By using levels of children's involvement, it has been a long held belief that as practitioners we can assess and plan to further engage them in deep learning.

References

Dahlberg, G. and Moss, P. (2005) *Ethics and Politics in Early Childhood Education*. London: Routledge-Falmer.

Dubiel, J. (2015) Being accountable for what really matters. Nursery World Conference presentation. Unpublished.

Laevers, F. (ed.) (1994) *The Leuven Involvement Scale for Young Children, LIS-YC*. Manual. Leuven, Belgium: Centre for Experiential Education.

Laevers, F. (1997) Assessing the quality of childcare provision. 'Involvement' as criterion. Available at: http://www.dauphin.be/Microsites%20Algemeen%20DOWNLOADS/CEGO/CEGOeng/pdf/Assesssing%20the%20quality%20of%20childcare%20provision.pdf (accessed 9 September, 2014).

Laevers, F. (2002) The quality of early childhood education. What we can learn from practice and research in Flanders. In Laevers, F. *Research on Experiential Education Reader*. Leuven, Belgium: Centre for Experiential Education.

Laevers, F. (2005) *Deep-level Learning and the Experiential Approach in Early Childhood and Primary Education*. Leuven, Belgium: Katholieke Universiteit Leuven, Research Centre for Early Childhood and Primary Education.

Laevers, F. (2007) Deep level learning. An exemplary application on the area of physical knowledge. *European Early Childhood Education Research Journal*, 1(1): 53–68.

Laevers, F. (2009) Interview with Ferre Laevers from the Scottish Learning Festival 2009. Available at: http://www.educationscotland.gov.uk/video/f/video_tcm4565868.asp (accessed 14 September, 2014).

Laevers, F., Bogaerts, M. and Moons, J. (1997) *Experiential Education at Work. A Setting with 5 Year Olds*. Manual. Leuven, Belgium: Centre for Experiential Education.

Nursery World Show and Conference (2015). Business Design Centre, Islington, London, 6–7 February.

Ofsted (2014) *Evaluation Schedule for Inspections of Registered Early Years Provision. Guidance and Grade Descriptors for Inspecting Registered Early Years Provision*. Ref. 120086. Manchester: Ofsted.

Pascal, C. and Bertram, A. (1997) *Effective Early Learning Project*. Worcester: Centre for Research in Early Childhood.

Pascal, C. and Bertram, A. (2005) *Baby Effective Early Learning Project*. Worcester: Amber Publications.

Rogoff, B. (1990) *Apprenticeship in Thinking. Cognitive Development in Social Context*. Oxford: Oxford University Press.

Rogoff, B., Goodman Turkanis, C. and Bartlett, L. (eds) (2001) *Learning Together. Children and Adults in a School Community*. Oxford: Oxford University Press.

Vygotsky, L. S. (1978) *Mind in Society*. Cambridge, MA: Harvard University Press.

Wiltshire County Council (nd) So what's so special about early years? Available at: http://education.wiltshire.gov.uk/html/early_years.html (accessed 21 September, 2015).

Chapter 1

Why involvement?

Annie Woods

All of you use a range of observation methods and techniques to help you support the learning of young children. You have developed these skills during your time as students, practitioners and parents. Some of you will be students just beginning to understand both why and how child observation is the key to effective planning for the environment you provide, the interventions you may make, and above all, the amazing developmental progress that children demonstrate, which you share with their parents. Some of you will also be managers and advisors, helping practitioners to use a range of tools for the observation and assessment of children and providing the means to sustain and enhance high quality early years care and education; indeed, it is very rare when visiting settings and talking with practitioners that the term *levels of involvement* has not been heard of, recognised, used or fully integrated into assessment practice. What is perhaps less clear, is the extent to which we all understand why and how the Leuven Involvement Scales of Involvement for Young Children (LIS-YC) have become such an important and international aspect of our work as early years practitioners.

In this chapter, a professional and personal examination of Laevers' research and practice is presented to deepen and further inform our practice as effective practitioners, and a range of theoretical ideas that appear to inform the practice of looking for and acting upon the levels of involvement in individual and groups of children is considered. The aim is to explore how Laevers' work is both informed by researchers and theorists and continues to inform current practice. The clarity and eloquence with which Laevers expresses his ideas, which some of you will have heard first-hand, is exploited through longer references than perhaps would be usual in a chapter because Laevers *continues* to work, write, advise and research. In addition, Laevers' concept of experiential education will be considered, as this is an important and continuing aspect of his work and not always explored fully by those of us 'cascading' the training of using the process-oriented approach to others.

In Chapter 2, we move from the *why* levels of involvement to the *how*: being involved in using the observational scales of involvement and the key element of reflective self-evaluation, as we deepen our effective practice and use the information gathered about the children in our provision to encourage their level of involvement by raising the quality of our environment.

Having taught students for many years, it has always been a privilege to encourage students to re-search the philosophical and pedagogical steps and journey that inform current thinking and practice with very young children; to comment upon and critique what Bruce (2005) would term 'the bedrock of the early childhood traditions'. It is through observational traditions that theoretical influences can be traced through Laevers' research papers, lectures, presentations and consultations with local authorities, advisory groups and Education Scotland, in Reggio Emilia and in New Zealand, with High Scope Educators and children's centres, and in the Research Centre for Experiential Education, Leuven University in Belgium.

Laevers and Heylen (2003: 13) write:

> In May 1976 twelve Flemish pre-school teachers, assisted by two educational consultants, start a series of sessions with the intention to reflect critically upon their practice. Their approach is 'experiential': the intention is to make a close, moment by moment description of what it means to a young child to live and take part in the educational setting.

Laevers adds, in 2011 (online):

> The educational model Experiential Education (EXE) evolved during the 1970s and 1980s, from a series of observations of young children in early education settings in Flanders, Belgium. Since that time, EXE has grown to become one of the most influential models in the area of early childhood education in Flanders and has been disseminated across a range of world regions and countries, including Australia, Croatia, Ecuador, Finland, France, Germany, Ireland, Japan, the Netherlands, Portugal, South Africa and the U.K. In sum, Experiential Education sees well-being and involvement as a measure of deep learning and of the effectiveness of the learning environment. Because these indicators of quality learning can be easily accessed by practitioners, the process-oriented strategy has an empowering impact on them and can help them to develop the huge potential of children. The approach has been further developed for child care, special education, secondary education, higher education and in service training.
>
> Research on quality at the level of the learner, EXE [Experiential Education] theory suggests that the most economical way to assess the quality of any educational setting (from preschool to adult education) – in particular, from the perspective of the learner – is to focus on two process dimensions: the 'emotional well-being' and the 'level of involvement' of the learner. 'Well-being' indicates that the basic needs of the child are satisfied and refers to the degree to which children feel at ease, act spontaneously, and show vitality and self-confidence. 'Involvement' is evident when children are concentrated and focused, interested and fascinated and when they are operating at the very limits of their capabilities.

As Whalley (2007: 58) suggests:

> Laevers' work is well established and rigorous, and it is particularly accessible to early years workers. Laevers has been looking at the processes of learning as well as the outcomes or products. He is interested in what is happening inside children as they learn.

Edwards *et al.* (2010: 136) concur:

> Process over product supports children's learning and knowledge acquisition. Process over product has been emphasised as an important component of learning, suggesting that the act of participation in play is more important than what the play itself generates.

Manning-Morton and Thorpe (2003: 110) also illuminate this point:

> [Laevers] has developed the LIS [Leuven Involvement Scale] as a means of assessing the effects of the learning situation on the child, by observing and rating the child's level of involvement in play according to certain defined signals. He describes involvement as a quality of human activity that can be recognised by concentration and persistence. It is characterised by motivation and fascination, openness to stimuli and intensity of experience both at the sensory and cognitive level.

When re-searching Laevers' ideas, a number of terms, ideas, concepts and themes are repeated and stressed, forming the bedrock of his theoretical approach and practice in examining children's learning and incorporated into signals and scales of involvement.

The language and ideas appear to reflect the theories and approaches of Piaget, Rogers and Maslow, Csíkszentmihályi, Dewey, Vygotsky, Bruner, Rogoff and Bronfenbrenner, alongside the observational work of Steiner, McMillan, Isaacs and Carr, and it is through these theorists that Laevers' work will be examined to support and deepen your understanding and appreciation 'on the importance of play, of observing and tuning into the "child-mind"' (Pound, 2011: 40). There will be few practitioners unfamiliar with the theorists or the language that pervade Laevers' published work.

Involvement

Laevers (2007a: 61) defines the concept of 'involvement' as

> a quality of human activity, characterised by concentration and persistence, a high level of motivation, intense perceptions and experiencing of meaning, a strong flow of energy, a high degree of satisfaction, and based on the exploratory drive and basic development of schemes. Involvement is a dimension of human activity. It is not linked to specific types of behaviour nor to specific levels of development.
>
> This high intensity of experience indicates a great deal of (mental) energy is being mobilised and used in a most efficient way. Furthermore, the activities reflect the level of functioning attained by this particular person. One cannot get involved in activities that are too easy or that require more developed capabilities. Involved persons are highly motivated. But we have to stress that the source of this motivation is the exploratory need, eagerness to understand and learn, the drive to get to grips with reality (in the literal and figurative sense of the word). Involvement always implicates intrinsic motivation.
>
> We hypothesise that this kind of activity leads (gradually or suddenly) to shifts in the fundamental schemes.

In reviewing the research of Ulich and Mayr (2003: 183) Laevers reiterates their conclusion that:

> involvement as a single concept 'is addressing motivational, emotional and cognitive aspects of a child's activity.' An involved person is narrowing his or her attention to a relatively limited (concentration). There is at the same time a tendency to continue

the activity (persistence). An involved person is fascinated and gives him (her) self completely (motivation). A generally acknowledged signal of this state is the distortion of time perception: time passes by without being noticed. At the level of cognitive functioning there is alertness and an openness to (relevant) stimuli. Perception is remarkably fresh and vivid and at the more abstract level of cognition, meanings are felt in an intensive way. The activity is accompanied by a bodily felt stream of positive energy and strong feeling of satisfaction. The source of this satisfaction is a complex of motives that comes down to the exploratory drive, the basic need to get a better grip on reality (intrinsic motivation). Further, involvement is situated at the verge of one's personal capabilities or in one's 'zone of proximal development'. An involved person uses the full potential of his/her capabilities. Finally, for all of the aspects mentioned in the definition, involvement is seen as an indication for developmental changes taking place, changes that have to be defined as deep level learning.

(Laevers, 1993)

We recognise many of these ideas in Laevers' (1994) LIS-YC signals of involvement (Table 1.1).

Laevers explains (Laevers' bold emphasis):

Children with a high level of involvement are highly **concentrated** and **absorbed** by their activity. They **show interest, motivation** and even fascination. That is why they tend to **persevere**. Their mimic[ry] and posture indicate **intense mental activity**. They fully experience sensations and meanings. A strong sense of **satisfaction** results from the fulfilment of their **exploratory** drive. When there is involvement we know children are operating at the very **limits of their capabilities**. Because of all these qualities involvement is the condition that brings about **deep level learning**.

(Laevers, 2005: 10)

The encounter below (Woods, 2013: 56) illustrates many of these aspects of absorption, concentration, interest and satisfaction over a period of 40 minutes; in addition, Freddie shows us how *affected* he was by the experience of the ladybird on his coat, giving it a voice and feelings. We can associate this learning with both Piaget's animism and Rogers' 'empathic understanding' of other (Rogers, 1983).

Encounter: The language of ladybirds

Freddie (with ladybird): He loves me. He wants to come home with me. (Voicing for ladybird) I can't fly as I have no wings. I can only be his pet. (To me) Why can ladybirds swap legs when they walk? Long way to climb up, maybe he can climb all the way up here. Wait and see. He can climb up my zip. He's never gonna fly off me. He can climb up the tree (lifts onto tree).

(Woods, 2013: 56)

Table 1.1 LIS-YC signals of involvement

Concentration
The child is narrowing his/her attention to the limited circle of his/her activity. Only intense stimuli can reach and maybe distract him/her. A main point of reference for the observer (with most activities) are the child's eye movements: are the eyes fixed on the material or do they occasionally wander?

Energy
In motor activities physical energy is involved. One could even regard the degree of transpiration as a measure for involvement. In other activities a physical component may still catch the eye: loud talking (shouting), the actions being carried out in a relatively short time. However, this must not be confused with the release of pent-up energy (e.g. because one had to be quiet for too long). Mental energy can become apparent in the zeal displayed in action or, more abstractly, in the (mental) effort showing on faces.

Complexity and creativity
Children are at their best in activities accompanied by involvement. These activities are matching their competence. They fully apply to their cognitive and other capabilities. As a result, their behaviour is more than a routine behaviour. More often than not complexity involves creativity: the child adds an individual touch to the activity, he/she brings in his/her elements, produces something new, shows something not entirely predictable, something personal.

Facial expression and posture
Non-verbal signals are a great help when assessing the level of involvement. It is, for instance, possible to distinguish between eyes staring dreamily into space, wandering from one point to the other, and an intense look. When stories are told feelings and moods can be told straight from the child's face. The overall posture can reveal high concentration or boredom. Even when children are seen from the back only, one might assess the level of (non) involvement.

Persistence
When concentrating, the child directs his full attention and energy towards one point. The child's persistence reflects the length of observed concentration. Children who are involved do not easily let go of the action. They want the sensation of satisfaction, experienced with intense activity, to last and they are quite willing to do the necessary efforts. They are not easily distracted by minor activities. Activities possessing the quality of involvement tend to last (subject to age and levels of development).

Precision
Involved children give special attention to their work: they are susceptible to details and show precision in their actions. Non-involved children tend to race through their work; they are negligent. In verbally oriented activities less obvious details escape their notice (casual words, gestures ...).

Reaction time
Young children are alert and easily respond to interesting stimuli. They actually jump to action (e.g. after several possible activities were introduced), thus expressing motivation. They also react to new stimuli occurring in the course of action, provided those are relevant.

Verbal utterances
Children sometimes explicitly indicate that they are/were involved by their spontaneous comments ('I liked that!'; 'Can we do that again?') They can also indicate more implicitly that the activity appeals to them by giving enthusiastic descriptions of what they are/have been doing: they cannot refrain from putting into words what they are experiencing, discovering ...

Satisfaction
Activities possessing the quality of involvement often induce a feeling of 'satisfaction'. The source of this feeling may vary, but it must always imply 'exploration', 'getting a grip on reality', 'responding to certain stimuli'. This feeling of satisfaction is often implicit, but sometimes one can notice a child looking with utter satisfaction at his/her work, touching it ....

© LIS-YC signals of involvement (Laevers, 1994).

Piaget's influence

Freddie's 'mastery' and 'skill', accompanied by his focused patience with the ladybird, recall Piaget's theoretical observations. The signals of involvement appear to be 'based on a constructivist tradition [where] real learning affects the deeper structures on which competencies and dispositions are based' (Laevers, 2006: 20). In a later article Laevers alludes to:

> the concept of 'deep level learning' and raises two questions: when can we speak of real developmental changes and how do these occur? Referring to the constructivist tradition, the concept of 'basic scheme' is elaborated and the notions of 'assimilation' and 'accommodation' revisited. Further, 'involvement' is presented as a necessary condition for development.
>
> (Laevers, 2007a: 53)

He also cites Birns and Golden (1973) in his interpretation of the basic tenets of Piaget's theory:

> *'Assimilation is simply the application of an established behaviour pattern to a familiar or new situation. If the behaviour is successful, the child is not forced to change his behaviour in the new situation. However, if the behaviour is not successful, the child must adapt or change his behaviour to the new situation. Accommodation is changing an existing behaviour pattern that does not work in the new situation.'*
>
> The dynamic that urges a person to make accommodations is conceptualised in the notion of adaptation: the mental system strives towards an equilibrium. According to Piaget, the equilibrium sought is that between assimilation and accommodation.
>
> (Ibid.: 57)

Freddie, demonstrating high levels of involvement with 'his' ladybird, watches how the insect 'swaps' his legs as it walks, perhaps noticing for the first time that insects with six legs use opposing movements to climb and clamber when not flying. Freddie has watched ladybirds walking on leaves as well as flying from plant to plant. He now has to assimilate new knowledge of how six, rather than his own two, legs work and may in future accommodate this new learning to other four- and six-legged creatures and adapt it when watching spiders, for example. During the period in the woodland with Freddie, his abiding interest was with insects, and Laevers (2007a: 59) reminds us that 'Piagetians generally advocate the stimulation of child activity by giving a rich environment and room for free initiative and rewarding the production of "wonderful ideas" (Duckworth, 1979; after Hohman *et al.*, 1979)'. Moran, in Chapter 4 considers how the outside can stimulate high levels of involvement.

We are unable to subscribe Freddie with a recognised schema pattern, but his absorbed play with ladybirds (Woods, 2013: 56) suggests his 'scheme' or understanding of their movements is under development and being refined, and crucially, being observed. Pound (2011: 38, 47) reminds us that:

Observation is an important part of the work of the adult. Steiner Waldorf Education (2009) refers to observation as 'picture building ... and the detailed and extensive observations collected during her time at the Malting House underpinned Isaacs' subsequent theories and writings.

Piaget and Isaacs both observed children in action in order to discern the learning *process*: 'in short, intelligenta functioning, when equilibria obtained, is made up of a balanced recipe of about equal parts of assimilation and accommodation' (Flavell, 1963 in Laevers, 2007a: 57). Through play action, the child practices with what he knows, explores new ideas and possibilities and applies or connects other experiences to the play, and, if satisfyingly challenging, reaches a new understanding or balance. For Laevers, these observable actions demonstrate high levels of involvement and deep level learning. Gardner (2006: 17) suggests:

> Piaget's overall model of the child as an active problem solver has carried the day. Piaget not only put the serious study of the child on the scientific map, but also moved the child's cognitive powers to the forefront, where they have firmly remained.

The problem-solving child

Laevers and Piaget see the active, involved child as one who perseveres with an activity, problem, or challenge and sees it through to a satisfactory, self-determined outcome. In suggesting a synthesis of theories present in Laevers' current ideas, the notion of the problem-solving child appears to also find a good fit with Rogers' person-centred theory developed during his practice as a psychoanalyst. Pound (2011: 83) suggests:

> Rogers referred to the fully functioning person. Both concepts require mental health and psychological well-being. The aim of teaching, Rogers suggests, is to support the development of fully-functioning people. He focused on the role of teachers in facilitating learning through empathy and through creating a climate which allowed *freedom to learn*. (Curzon 2003). He favoured experiential learning over direct instruction. For him experiential education included:
>
> - The personal involvement of the learner;
> - An excitement which stimulated both feeling and cognition;
> - Self-initiated learning;
> - Learning based on meaning.
>
> (Based on Curzon 2003: 117)

Pound (2011: 84) also implies that Laevers has assimilated his ideas:

> Rogers' theories suggest that an assessment of process is key to the work of parents and educators (Kramer, 1995) and are readily understood by many early childhood educators. This may be because they chime with many other, more familiar, theories.

It may be argued that Rogers' 'fully functioning person' is accommodated into Laevers' identification of a highly involved child or adult. He states:

> An exploratory attitude, defined by openness for, and alertness to, the wide variety of stimuli that form our surroundings, makes a person accessible, lowers the threshold for getting into the state of 'arousal' that brings a person into the most intense forms of concentration and involvement.
>
> (Laevers, 2006: 21)

Further:

> Involvement is not, however, the state of arousal easily obtained by the entertainer. The crucial point is that the satisfaction that goes along with involvement stems from one source, the exploratory drive, the need to get a better grip on reality, the intrinsic interest in how things and people are, the urge to experience and figure out.
>
> (Ibid.: 24)

If we compare Laevers' approach to Rogers' (1983) research, narrated in one of his last collection of essays, there appears to be a strong resonance. It is useful to consider a lengthy reference to Rogers where he claims that:

> [significant or experiential learning] *has a quality of personal involvement* – the whole person in both feeling and cognitive aspects being *in* the learning event. It is *self-initiated*. Even when the impetus or stimulus comes from the outside, the sense of discovery, of reaching out, of grasping and comprehending, comes from within. *It is pervasive*. It makes a difference in the behaviour, the attitudes, perhaps even the personality of the learner. *It is evaluated by the learner*. One knows whether it is meeting her need, whether it leads towards what she wants to know, whether it illuminates the dark area of ignorance she is experiencing. The locus of evaluation, we might say, resides definitely in the learner. *Its essence is meaning*. When such learning takes place, the elements of meaning to the learner is built into the whole experience (p. 20).

> It appears that the person who emerges from a theoretically optimal experience of personal growth … through experience of learning and development, is then a fully functioning person. He is able to live fully in and with each and all of his feelings and reactions. He is his own sifter of evidence, but is open to evidence from all sources; he is completely engaged in the process of being and becoming himself, and thus discovers that he is soundly and realistically social; he lives completely in this moment … (p. 290)
>
> (Rogers, 1983)

Wardle and Vesty (in Woods, 2014: 35) consider many aspects of well-being and motivation and the following encounter reflects both the absorption and evaluation of the learner.

Encounter: Intrinsic motivation

Mary, who is 18 months old is sitting by herself and playing with a set of plastic saucepans. One saucepan has a lid that fits on it perfectly and Mary is trying to put the lid on to the various saucepans. At first she tries to put the lid onto the two smaller saucepans but seeing it will not fit she then turns to the third saucepan, which is the correct saucepan for the lid. Mary sits very quietly on her own turning the lid around to attempt to fit it to the saucepan perfectly. She is totally engrossed in this task, sometimes the lid goes inside the pan, other times she puts it on but it falls off. Mary continues to attempt this task for five minutes just sitting on her own determined to get the lid onto the saucepan correctly. Finally the lid snaps on perfectly in place onto the pan and Mary knows that this is the right fit. At this point she looks up and sees that there is an adult observing her and so she smiles and starts to clap herself.

(in Woods, 2014: 35)

Not only do Laevers' ideas resonate with Rogers' fully functioning person, but also Maslow's primary need for self-actualisation. We can further associate learner evaluation with our understanding of metacognition: Mary is self-directed, motivated, problem-solving, absorbed and persevering, assimilating new 'fitting' schema and adapting her skills. When she 'meets' the pots and lids again, she is likely to recall this play *and her success,* and will complete the task more quickly because she knows how to be successful. She will recall 'the knowing'. There is an element of creativity and intuition involved with the processes of deep level learning. Mary *knows* it is the right fit; Laevers (2006: 21) suggests that: 'Intuition is "the faculty to mentally represent reality, making use of one's imagination, by which meanings are reconstructed", enabling one to get the "feel" of the real thing.'

Rogers used the phrase 'being and becoming', and Pound (2011) recognises his continued influence in the strands of Te Whāriki (Ministry of Education, 1996). Laevers, in a keynote speech (Laevers and Heylen, 2003: 3), 'felt there is something in common between Experiential Education, Te Whāriki, High Scope and Reggio Emilia'. Laevers (2005: 2–3) warns (my italics for emphasis):

A lot of effort within the area of education is content based. That explains why, generally, the disposition of curiosity or, in a broader sense, the exploratory drive, doesn't get as much attention as it deserves. Investing in the preservation or even strengthening of the exploratory drive can be seen as most rewarding in so far as it *guarantees lifelong learning.* An exploratory attitude, defined by openness for, and alertness to the wide variety of stimuli that form our surroundings, makes a person accessible, lowers the threshold for getting into the state of 'arousal' that brings a person to the most intense forms of concentration and involvement. *That person will never stop developing.* The challenge for education is not only to keep this intrinsic source of motivation alive, but also to make it encompass all domains that belong to reality.

Creativity goes beyond this. It is defined as the 'disposition to produce many unique ideas appropriate to a simple problem requirement'. In further analysis the component of 'ideational fluency' is decisive: the easiness with which associations are made which link distant elements to one another. These combinations are original and at the same time purposeful. Associated with this disposition is the *continuing tendency* to look at things from different angles, to be flexible, to be humorous (as a way to 'play' with reality) … and to risk getting into conflict with ones surroundings, because new ideas can mean a threat to the existing order.

Gradually a third factor caught our attention: the competence of *self-organisation*. We define it as 'the managerial capacity to organise one's life in a way that makes the best possible use of the available resources, in oneself (own competencies, limitations and strengths) and in one's human and physical environment. We discern four components: will-power or the capacity to be determined and commit oneself to something, the capability to make choices and to sort out what one really wants, the capability to reproduce scenarios for action and develop them further while the activity is going on and the capability to step back and reassess the situation in view of one's goals.

Deep level learning leads to a kind of paradigm shift through which more of the complexities of the world (in whatever domain) can be experienced and become meaningful. In our reflection on the essence of the process of cognition a form of intelligence based on intuitive faculties, as opposed to the logical-mathematical intelligence, came to the foreground. We see intuition as the basis for real understanding of the world …

It is argued, therefore, that Laevers is interested in the possibilities encountered by the learner and how that shapes and influences future developmental opportunities, both for the child and the adults facilitating that development.

Csíkszentmihályi's state of flow

A further thread that is influenced by Rogers and woven through these approaches is the idea of 'flow'. In many of Laevers' presentations and research articles (1997; 2000; 2005; 2007a,b; 2011; Laevers and Heylen, 2003) and first alluded to in 1997 by Pascal and Bertram, he refers to the 'state of flow'.

Csíkszentmihályi (1979) speaks of 'the state of flow'. One of the most predominant characteristics of this flow state is concentration. An involved person narrows his attention to one limited circle. Involvement goes along with strong motivation, fascination and total implication; there is no distance between person and activity, no calculation of possible benefits. Furthermore there is an openness to (relevant) stimuli and the perceptual and cognitive functioning has an intensity which is lacking in other kinds of activity. The meanings of words and ideas are felt more strongly and deeply. Further analysis reveals a manifest feeling of satisfaction and a stream of energy felt through the body. People actively seek this 'state of flow'. Young children usually find it in play.

(Laevers, 2006: 24)

Maslow's self-actualisation, Rogers' fully functioning person and Csíkszentmihályi's 'optimal experience' appear to complement Laevers' experiential approach. Csíkszentmihályi (2002: 4) states: 'I developed a theory of optimal experience based on the concept of *flow* – the state in which people are so involved in an activity that nothing else seems to matter.' He lists eight major components:

1   The experience usually occurs when we confront tasks we have a chance of completing.
2   We must be able to concentrate on what we are doing.
3   The concentration is usually possible because the task undertaken has clear goals
4   And provides immediate feedback.
5   One acts with a deep but effortless involvement that removes from awareness the worries and frustrations of everyday life.
6   Enjoyable experiences allow people to exercise a sense of control over their actions.
7   Concern for the self disappears, yet paradoxically the sense of self emerges stronger after the flow experience is over.
8   The sense of duration of time is altered.

(Csíkszentmihályi, 2002: 49)

The signals of involvement (seen in Table 1.1) appear to reflect these components closely. Many of the deep level learning concepts are encapsulated into Duffy's (1998) ideas to support imagination and creativity and Cremin *et al.*'s (2006) possibility thinking, representing a post-modernist approach to early years education; 'viewing the child as existing through its relations with others and always in a particular context' (Dahlberg *et al.*, 2007: 43). For post-modernists, there is no one universal truth or theory that can explain the child, childhood or their development.

Looking back at the encounters with Freddie and Mary,

one of the most universal and distinctive features of optimal experience takes place: people become so involved in what they are doing that the activity becomes spontaneous, almost automatic; they stop being aware of themselves as separate from the actions they are performing. Although the flow experience appears to be effortless, it often requires strenuous physical exertion, or highly disciplined mental activity. It does not happen without the application of skilled performance. Any lapse in concentration will erase it. And yet while it lasts consciousness works smoothly, action follows action seamlessly. There is one very important and at first apparently paradoxical relationship between losing the sense of self in a flow experience, and having it emerge stronger afterward. It almost seems that occasionally giving up self-consciousness is necessary for building a strong self-concept.

(Csíkszentmihályi, 2002: 53, 65)

Laevers uses the term *autotelic* to explain how deep level learning is seen within the relationship between the self and self-determined goal. Rogers (1961: 174) says of Maslow (1954):

Self-actualized people have a wonderful capacity to appreciate again and again, freshly and naively, the basic goods of life with awe, pleasure, wonder and even ecstasy, however stale these experiences may be for other people.

The good life is a *process,* not a state of being. It is a direction, not a destination. The direction which constitutes the good life is that which is selected by the total organism where there is psychological freedom to move in any direction.

Csíkszentmihályi's book *Flow* is sub-titled 'The Classic Work on How to Achieve Happiness': 'the principles of a fulfilled life – one full of enjoyment and constantly growing in complexity – suggests ways to prepare ourselves for the difficult choices that tomorrow will bring' (2002: x). For Laevers, well-being and happiness associated with children's curiosity, flexibility and inventiveness, *should* underpin what we want from education for our youngest children, where they are given many opportunities and autonomy to set and meet their own challenging goals within an empowering environment.

Experiential education

Deep level learning, high levels of involvement, strong self-concept and well-being: all elements of experiential education. Tenenbaum, writing in Rogers (1961, 1983: 302) suggested Rogers was influenced by Dewey, 'to think independently, creatively; to become deeply involved with their persons, their very selves'. Pound (2011: 110) cites Graham (2009), pointing out that:

The Plowden Report cited Piaget as the source of the view that children needed active experience in handling materials if they were to learn effectively, but in fact Susan Isaacs, following John Dewey, had made this a central feature of her educational philosophy well before Piaget considered the educational implications of his work.

Laevers (2006: 28) defines experiential education as

exploiting and enhancing the energy in people and drawing them into a positive spiral which engenders deep level learning. Only in this way can we make schools more effective and strong enough to meet the challenge of education: the development of adults who are self-confident and mentally healthy, curious and exploratory, expressive and communicative, imaginative and creative, full of initiative, well-organised, with articulated intuitions about the social and physical world and with a feeling of being connected to the universe and all its creatures.

Having 'an experience' for Dewey suggests

every successive part flows freely, without seam and without unfilled blanks into what ensues … In an experience, flow is from something to something … is so rounded out that its close is a consummation and not a cessation … the activity of the child takes on a quality of wholeness and completion, those moments when self and material fuse and together become the essence of the thing or situation. No one has ever watched a child intent in his play without being made aware of the complete merging of playfulness and seriousness.

(Cuffaro, 1995: 59, 85 cites Dewey's later works)

Dewey first suggested in 1910 what may have developed into Csíkszentmihályi's 'state of flow':

> Daydreaming, building of castles in the air, that loose flux of casual and disconnected material that floats through our minds in relaxed moments are, in this random sense, *thinking*. Reflection involves not simply a sequence of ideas, but a *consequence* – a consecutive ordering in such a way that each determines the next as its proper outcome, while each in turn leans back on its predecessors. Each phase is a step from something – technically speaking, it is a term of thought. The stream of flow becomes a train, chain or thread.
>
> (Dewey, 1910: 2–3)

He precedes Piaget when talking about

> the curious mind … constantly alert and exploring, seeking material for thought. Eagerness for experience, for new and varied contacts, is found where wonder is found. A physiological uneasiness leads a child to be 'into everything' – to be reaching, poking, pounding, prying. The most casual notice of the activities of a young child reveals a ceaseless display of exploring and testing activity.
>
> (Ibid.: 31)

Arnold (2003) reminds us that, in 1996, Csíkszentmihályi argued:

> Creativity is a central source of meaning in our lives … most of the things that are interesting, important and *human* are the results of creativity' (p.1). He goes on to say that creativity is what separates humans from animals. He finds creativity 'fascinating' because when we are involved in it, we feel that we are living more fully than during the rest of life' (p. 2). If too few opportunities for curiosity are available, if too many obstacles are placed in the way of risk and exploration, the motive to engage in creative behaviour is easily extinguished (p. 11).

Creative behaviour, alert, unique, and absorbed is

> transformed into interest in *problems* provoked by the observation of things and the accumulation of material. When the child continues to entertain it in his own mind and to be alert for whatever will help answer it, curiosity has become a positive intellectual force.
>
> (Dewey, 1910: 33)

For Laevers, experiential education affords a child, groups of children and adults the opportunity to be engaged, challenged and extended.

Dewey's philosophy is recalled here:

> … the person in Dewey's philosophy requires involvement with process, time, space, and histories, since forces and qualities remain lifeless unless elicited through interaction in the events and situations of the environment – an environment that exists, is there, while also is created and transformed through interaction. The person is 'in' as well as 'of' the environment.
>
> (Cuffaro, 1995: 16)

Encounter: Penny and the snails

1   Asking Penny why she liked snails so much. She said it was the circles, her favourite being the brown, white and black stripes. Ah, I replied, the stripe pattern was a spiral. 'Yes, I like the spirals'. Penny sustained her interest in snails, repaying the adults with evidence of deep engagement.

2   For the past three weeks, Penny has set about finding, holding and examining snails. She also picks up slugs and now knows that slugs do not live in shells but excrete slime to enable them to move. She finds very tiny snails and those with distinct patterns on their shells; she begins to notice the spiral pattern. When she picks them up, the snails go back into their shells and she wants them to crawl ... I make a suggestion that if she holds her hands still, the snail will usually emerge through warmth and stillness. Penny is too busy on the hunt for more snails and often deposits the found snails in my hand to 'warm them up'. Once emerged, she usually places them on a tree for safety and then is surprised at how far they can climb. Last week, Michael, caught up in her interest, spent a long time creating a nested bed for the snails and they both placed all the found snails on a log disc before covering them in dry leaves.

(Woods, 2014: 91)

Experiential education, the opportunity to 'go with the flow'; spiral patterns seen in shells, slime on hands, a snail's energetic climb; unplanned but an anticipated possibility, an adult 'ready, willing and able' to support and follow a child's interest. 'The project, still in progress, is regarded in Flanders and in the Netherlands as one of the most influential innovative movements of the nineties in the field of early childhood and primary education' (Laevers and Heylen, 2003: 7). Laevers' concern is that 'too many opportunities to sustain children's development remain unused' (ibid.: 13).

Positive spiral

Problem-solving, challenges, transformation of ideas and objects, and support from engaged and energetic adults underpin characteristics of effective learning. Laevers (in Robson, 2012: 116) states that 'involvement only occurs in the small area in which the activity matches the capabilities of the person that is in the "zone of proximal development"'. Levels of involvement, like ZPD are part of our early years lexicon; Bruner's spiral curriculum, Rogoff's guided participation and Vygotsky's co-construction are embedded in Laevers' thinking. Children do need to be challenged. Involvement only occurs somewhere between 'being able to do something' and 'not yet being able to do something'; 'understanding something' and 'being on the verge of understanding' (Laevers, 1997: 20). Piaget understood that children learn through assimilating actions and ideas and adapting them when meeting a new experience, which adds to their experience; sometimes the challenging 'event' will provoke a disequilibrium, an imbalance between what we think we know and understand. Laevers (2007a: 59–60) states:

The consequence for practice is that we have to provide activities that require behaviour only slightly different from and slightly more demanding than the ones already available in the child's repertoire. Teachers have to use this 'optimal discrepancy' as a guideline for intervention.

In Dewey's (1910: 33–34) words: 'the teacher has usually more to learn than to teach, … to keep alive the sacred spark of wonder and to fan the flame that already glows'. Pascal and Bertram (1997: 5) identify that Laevers' 'project draws fundamentally on the importance of the social context of children's learning.' Csíkszentmihályi (1992) had claimed previously that the 'state of flow' is reached when children's skills and abilities are matched to activities 'at the edge of their capabilities' (Laevers, 1993, 1996 in Pascal and Bertram, 1997: 6). Links to Vygotskian theory are also considered by Ulrich and Mayr (in Laevers and Heylen, 2003: 29):

> Involvement is clearly related to theories of intrinsic motivation and the concept of interest. High involvement in a teacher-directed activity means that the activity has been transformed by the child into a personally meaningful and interesting event. Interest theory has not merely focused on individual relatively stable interest domains, but also on task-orientated situational interest and the latter is closely related to the concept of involvement.

Their research supports Laevers' (2011, online) research, which established that:

> involvement is situated at the verge of one's personal capabilities or in one's 'zone of proximal development'. An involved person uses the full potential of his/her capabilities. Finally, for all of the aspects mentioned in the definition, involvement is seen as an indication for developmental changes taking place, changes that have to be defined as deep level learning (Laevers, 1993). The key concept of involvement in a sense guarantees that something very valuable is going on in the child, here and now, something that inevitably must lead to deep level learning, within the area of competences addressed in the activity at stake.

This 'intense proximal process' (Bronfenbrenner and Ceci, 1994: 572, cited in Declercq et al., 2011: 65) is the basis of Laevers' continued research. It recalls the work at High Scope and in Reggio Emilia. Malaguzzi (in Edwards et al., 1998: 81) reminds us that:

> [Children] are autonomously capable of making meaning from their daily life experiences through mental acts involving planning, coordination of ideas, and abstraction. Remember, meanings are never static, univocal or final; they are always generative of other meanings. The central act of adults, therefore is to activate, especially indirectly, the meaning making competencies of children as a basis of all learning.

Dewey, Rogers and Laevers urge us to observe, listen, reflect, respond, provoke, guide and help both children's transformations of ideas and objects in a holistic approach, reminding us of Bronfenbrenner's dynamic ideas of social construction.

Ecological systems theory

Albon (in Miller and Pound, 2011: 40–41) argues that:

> Knowledge is socially constructed; it is contingent on culture, time and space. It can never be value-free and objective. It is possible for little narratives to develop to reflect the thinking of smaller communities and contingent on their particular socio-cultural understandings. It is a theory that embraces diversity, uncertainty and complexity.

A child learns within a number of environments created by communities; activities and experiences are encountered, absorbed, recalled, and shaped. Dahlberg *et al.*, mentioned earlier in the chapter, state 'the world and our knowledge of it are seen as *socially constructed* and all of us, as human beings, are active participants in this process ... engaged in relationships with others in meaning making rather than truth finding' (Dahlberg *et al.*, 2007: 23). Of meaning making, Dewey (1910: 57) suggests 'we naturally use the words *weigh, ponder* [and] *deliberate*. Closely related names are *scrutiny, examination, consideration, inspection* – terms which imply close and careful vision'. This may be a seven-week-old baby beginning to find her thumb, bringing her little right fist to her mouth, at first seemingly haphazard, but after repeating this action many times, whenever she is lying on her back, a sensory schema is forming. Out of the immediate family circle, it may be a toddler preferring to lie on the floor to fit a large floor puzzle in a church hall on his own for the first time. It could be a six-year-old who recognises logos and his name and the shape of titles of books, but does not appear to be able to read new words, suddenly finding interest in a world cup chart of flags and teams: 'eureka' – I can read! The ten-year-old girl who has played with floating and sinking objects but can now rationalise why a large surface metal object will float if it is large enough – like a tanker. The baby has been afforded the possibility of playing independently; the toddler has been encouraged to complete a puzzle on the floor; a six-year-old has had his interests met and they appropriately meet his developing reading needs and the ten year old has experienced playing with water, sorting objects, devising experiments. Laevers (2007b: 23–24) states:

> It certainly is endorsed by the social constructivist view: meaning is shaped through communication. Learning therefore is a joint activity, a collaborative act.
>
> Mental representation is about what Aebli (1963) called 'die geistige Kraft' – the power of the mind, the faculty to create a felt sense, the feel of meanings ranging from the physical experience up to the representation of the more abstract constructions and concepts such as 'creativity', 'intelligence', 'synergy', 'constructivism'.

In essence, Laevers' research alludes to Bronfenbrenner's theory of human development, 'defined ... as a lasting change in the way which a person perceives and deals with his environment ... and the evolving interaction between the two' (Bronfenbrenner, 1979: 3). As Van Sanden and Joly (in Laevers and Heylen, 2003: 146) argue:

> Well-being and involvement are not really properties or fixed characteristics of the child itself. They do give an indication of the interaction between the child's characteristics on the one hand and the environment's properties on the other hand.

If this interaction is positive, in other words, if the teacher succeeds in tuning in to the child's specific needs, this will result in a high level of well-being and involvement. If the interaction is negative, the setting is not (sufficiently) tuned into the child's needs, which will result in a low level of well-being and involvement.

Where the child/children, parents, practitioner, environment dynamic is nurturing, attuned, appropriately challenging and effective, it 'demands active participation of the child who, in his or her response and initiative, will flag what kind of impulse he/she needs at this very moment' (Laevers, 2007b: 26). He adds:

> The rationale implicated here rests on the experiential view on learning and development, a view that respects the dynamics of development because it suggests that intense (mental) activity in a particular domain ('involvement') is a necessary and sufficient condition to provoke changes at the level of basic schemes that will affect the whole functioning of a person in that particular area (see Laevers, 1998). That is what deep level learning is about: not just adding a file but getting into the program and upgrading it.
>
> (Ibid.: 27)

In Chapter 2, our understanding of deep level learning is considered through discussion of a research 'snapshot' and by focusing on the processes of experiences as described by Laevers:

> Experiences accumulated in the EXE project support the conclusion that well-being and involvement are welcomed by practitioners as most stimulating and helpful to improve the quality of their work. The concepts of well-being and involvement match the intuitions of many caretakers and teachers and give them a scientifically-based confirmation of what they knew already: when we can get children in that 'flow state', development must and will take place within the area(s) addressed by the activity. In contrast to effect variables – the real outcomes are only seen on the longer run – the process variables give immediate feedback about the quality of interventions and tell us on the spot something about their potential impact. Furthermore, bringing at the foreground involvement as key indicator for quality, engenders a lot of positive energy and synergy: the enthusiastic responses of children, when teaching efforts are successful, are very empowering and give the teacher deep satisfaction both at the professional and the personal level. Finally, taking involvement as a point of reference in the guidance of professionals makes it possible to respect the actual level of functioning of the teacher and the setting.
>
> (Laevers, 2005: 8)

Provocations

- In team meetings, how often and to what extent do you express confidence in basing your discussions about children from different theoretical perspectives?
- Team members undergoing further professional development and students on placement will be reflecting upon theorists in their studies; in what ways could you empower them to contribute to developing your community of practice?

- In what ways do you share training events, conferences or network meetings to sustain effective learning as adults?
- When did you last discuss a child's repeated pattern of behaviour (schema), signals of involvement and zones of proximal development when discussing children and your possible plans for future activities?
- Recall the last time you saw a child 'in flow'? What were they doing and how could you share this type of observation with a parent?

References

Arnold, C. (2003) *Observing Harry. Child Development and Learning 0–5*. Maidenhead: Open University Press.

Bronfenbrenner, U. (1979) *The Ecology of Human Development. Experiments by Nature and Design*. Cambridge, MA: Harvard University Press.

Bruce, T. (2005) *Early Childhood Education*. 3rd edn. London: Hodder Arnold.

Cremin, T., Burnard, P. and Craft, A. (2006). Pedagogy and possibility thinking in the early years. *Journal of Thinking Skills and Creativity*, 1(2): 108–119.

Csíkszentmihályi, M. (1992) *Flow. The Classic Work on How to Achieve Happiness*. 2nd edn. New York: Harper & Row.

Csíkszentmihályi, M. (2002) *Flow. The Classic Work on How to Achieve Happiness*. 2nd edn. New York: Harper & Row.

Cuffaro, H.K. (1995) *Experimenting with the World. John Dewey and the Early Childhood Classroom*. New York: Teachers College Press.

Dahlberg, G., Moss, P. and Pence, A. (2007) *Beyond Quality in Early Childhood Education Care and Education*. London: Routledge.

Declercq, B., Ebrahim, H., Koen, M., Martin, C., van Zyl, E., Daries, G. *et al.* (2011) Levels of well-being and involvement of young children in centre-based provision in the Free State Province of South Africa. *South African Journal of Childhood Education*, 1(2): 64–80.

Dewey, J. (1910) *How We Think*. Boston, MA: Heath and Co.

Duffy, B. (1998) *Supporting Creativity and Imagination in the Early Years*. Maidenhead: Open University Press.

Edwards, C., Gandini, L. and Forman, G. (eds) (1998) *The Hundred Languages of Children. The Reggio Emilia Approach – Advanced Reflections*. 2nd edn. Westport, CT: Ablex Publishing.

Edwards, S., Cutter-Mackenzie, A. N. and Hunt, E. (2010) Framing play for learning. Professional reflections on the role of open-ended play in early childhood education. In Brooker, L. and Edwards, S. (eds) *Engaging Play*. Maidenhead: Open University Press, Chapter 10.

Gardner, H. (2006) *The Development and Education of the Mind. The Selected Works of Howard Gardner*. London: Routledge.

Laevers, F. (1993). Deep level learning. An exemplary application on the area of physical knowledge. *European Early Childhood Education Research Journal*, 1(1): 53–68.

Laevers, F. (ed.) (1994) *The Leuven Involvement Scale for Young Children, LIS-YC*. Manual. Leuven, Belgium: Centre for Experiential Education.

Laevers, F. (1997) Assessing the quality of childcare provision. 'Involvement' as criterion. Available at: http://www.dauphin.be/Microsites%20Algemeen%20DOWNLOADS/CEGO/CEGOeng/pdf/Assesssing%20the%20quality%20of%20childcare%20provision.pdf (accessed 9 September, 2014).

Laevers, F. (2000) Forward to basics! Deep-level learning and the experiential approach. *Early Years*, 20(2): 20–29.

Laevers, F. (2005) *Deep-level Learning and the Experiential Approach in Early Childhood and Primary Education*. Leuven, Belgium: Katholieke Universiteit Leuven, Research Centre for Early Childhood and Primary Education.

Laevers, F. (2006) *Making Care and Education More Effective Through Wellbeing and Involvement. An Introduction to Experiential Education*. Belgium: Leuven Institute.

Laevers, F. (2007a) Deep level learning. An exemplary application on the area of physical knowledge. *European Early Childhood Education Research Journal*, 1(1): 53–68.

Laevers, F. (2007b) The curriculum as means to raise the quality of early childhood education. Implications for policy. *European Early Childhood Education Research Journal*, 13(1): 17–29.

Laevers F. (2011) Experiential education. Making care and education more effective through well-being and involvement. Bennett, J. (topic ed.). In Tremblay, R. E., Boivin, M., Peters, R. DeV. and Barr, R. G. (eds) *Encyclopedia on Early Childhood Development*. Montreal, Quebec: Centre of Excellence for Early Childhood Development and Strategic Knowledge Cluster on Early Child Development, pp. 1–5. Available at: http://www.child-encyclopedia.com/documents/LaeversANGxp1.pdf (accessed 26 August, 2014).

Laevers, F. and Heylen, L. (eds) (2003) *Involvement of Children and Teacher Style. Insights from an International Study on Experiential Education. Studia Paedagogica 35*. Leuven, Belgium: Leuven University Press.

Manning-Morton, J. and Thorpe, M. (2003) *Key Times for Play*. Maidenhead: Open University Press.

Miller, L. and Pound, L. (2011) *Theories and Approaches to Learning in the Early Years*. London: Sage.

Ministry of Education (1996) *Te Whāriki*. Wellington, New Zealand: Learning Media.

Pascal, C. and Bertram, T. (1997) *Effective Early Learning*. London: PCP.

Pound, L. (2011) *Influencing Early Childhood Education. Key Figures, Philosophies and Ideas*. Maidenhead: Open University Press.

Robson, S. (2012) *Developing Thinking and Understanding in Young Children. An Introduction for Students*. 2nd edn. London: Routledge.

Rogers, C. (1961) *On Becoming a Person. A Therapist's View of Psychotherapy*. Boston, MA: Houghton Mifflin.

Rogers, C. (1983) *Freedom to Learn for the 80's*. 2nd edn. Columbus, OH: Charles E. Merrill.

Whalley, M. and the Pen Green Centre Team (2007) *Involving Parents in their Children's Learning*. 2nd edn. London: Sage.

Woods, A. (ed.) (2013) *Child-initiated Play and Learning. Planning for Possibilities in the Early Years*. London: David Fulton.

Woods, A. (ed.) (2014) *The Characteristics of Effective Learning: Creating and Capturing the Possibilities in the Early Years*. London: David Fulton.

Chapter 2

Being involved in levelling

Annie Woods

When a pebble is dropped into a pool, ripples spread across the pool and become an ever-widening set of circles. When we observe a child, the same effect can be experienced: the initial 'splash' creates opportunities for discussion, direction, interpretation, provocation and ever wider possibilities. Pound (2011: 109) cites Smith (2001) who recalls that 'Piaget recommended that teachers should be investigative in carrying out their assessments', and we can see, in this chapter, to what extent Laevers connected both an approach to observation and the imperative to support ongoing professional research and development. He says:

> Experiences accumulated in the EXE project support the conclusion that well-being and involvement are welcomed by practitioners as most stimulating and helpful to improve the quality of their work. The concepts of well-being and involvement match the intuitions of many caretakers and teachers and give them a scientifically-based confirmation of *what they knew already* [my italics]: when we can get children in that 'flow state', development must and will take place within the area(s) addressed by the activity. In contrast to effect variables – the real outcomes are only seen on the longer run – the process variables give immediate feedback about the quality of interventions and tell us on the spot something about their potential impact. Furthermore, bringing at the foreground involvement as key indicator for quality, engenders a lot of positive energy and synergy: the enthusiastic responses of children, when teaching efforts are successful, are very empowering and give the teacher deep satisfaction both at the professional and the personal level. Finally, taking involvement as a point of reference in the guidance of professionals makes it possible to respect the actual level of functioning of the teacher and the setting.
>
> When implementing experiential education, one starts where one stands, with the room, the children, the material, the books, the methods and all the limitations linked to the actual situation. The curriculum and all developmental domains are part of this environment. Then a field of action is chosen focusing on areas or groups of children showing low levels of involvement in systematic observations. Within the area(s) chosen, initiatives are taken which have the potential to bring about an increase in well-being and/or involvement. This increase – however small it may be – is experienced as a success and drives one towards new initiatives.
>
> (Laevers, 2000: 28)

This chapter aims to consider the practical instrument of LIS–YC, the signals and levels we look for when evaluating children's involvement in activities and how using the tool enriches discussion, reflection and the quality of the environmental possibilities we plan and provide for young children. The perception of quality and drive to improve quality in the early years through a number of initiatives and audits worldwide has meant that this instrument has been introduced in many settings by, for example, many English local authorities committed to the raising of quality in early years care and education settings. Recollections as an assistant head and foundation stage co-ordinator using this tool and a brief research exercise with a landscape architect will inform this chapter.

Introduction to scales of involvement

A very small pebble was thrown into the 'pond' of a church hall based pre-school one morning and the emerging ripples from this opportunity are presented to illustrate the potential of shared professional dialogue about a child, and an environment observed, with one staff member's thoughts and ideas resulting from the morning's reflection. As Rogoff (1990: 199) states:

> The mutual involvement of people working on similar issues is part of the social context of creativity. Dialogue, collaboration, and building from previous approaches often provide the catalyst for putting two ideas together that would not have occurred without the need for the individual thinker to carry out, explain, or improve on an approach.

In an interview with Education Scotland in 2009, Laevers talked about his early work in 1976:

> Quite quickly in the work with these teachers we understood that there is something that all teachers all over the world can understand very easily. And that is, if what you do is leading to wellbeing in children and higher levels of involvement, you are doing a good job. But once you go to wellbeing and involvement, of course you measure – and we have a very simple five-point scale for that, to measure wellbeing on the one hand, involvement on the other hand. And we did that a lot now, starting with babies and toddlers up to primary, secondary, higher education and adult education as well.

It is useful, here, to remind ourselves of the instrument designed by Laevers and the Research Centre for Experiential Education, Leuven University (Table 2.1).

The English translation of the LIS–YC 'package' was published in 1994, and consisted of two components: a manual and a video.

> It contains a detailed description of the scale rates and signals. In addition to this, our supervising experiences have enabled us to give concrete directions for the use of the scale as well as for the supervision of training sessions. This package offers a firm base for instructive sessions and team discussions and will help to develop observational and interpretative competencies with regard to one of the most powerful indicators of quality: the intensity of the child's activity or his involvement.
>
> (Laevers, 1994: 3)

Table 2.1 A process-oriented Self-evaluation Instrument for Care Settings

The scale for involvement

Level	Involvement	Examples
1	**Extremely low**	The child hardly shows any activity: • no concentration: staring, daydreaming; • an absent, passive attitude; • no goal-oriented activity; aimless actions, not producing anything; • no signs of exploration and interest; • not taking anything in, no mental activity.
2	**Low**	The child shows some degree of activity but [this] is often interrupted: • limited concentration; looks away during the activity; fiddles, dreams; • is easily distracted; • action only leads to limited results.
3	**Moderate**	The child is busy the whole time, but without real concentration: • routine actions, attention is superficial; • is not absorbed in the activity, activities are short lived; • limited motivation, no real dedication, does not feel challenged; • the child does not gain deep-level experiences; • does not use his/her capabilities to full extent; • the activity does not address the child's imagination.
4	**High**	There are clear signs of involvement, but these are not always present to their full extent: • the child is engaged in the activity without interruption; • most of the time there is real concentration, but during some brief moments the attention is more superficial; • the child feels challenged, there is a certain degree of motivation; • the child's capabilities and its imagination to a certain extent are addressed in the activity.
5	**Extremely high**	During the episode of observation the child is continuously engaged in the activity and completely absorbed in it: • is absolutely focused, concentrated without interruption; • is highly motivated, feels strongly [attracted] by the activity, perseveres; • even strong stimuli cannot distract him/her; • is alert, has attention for details, shows precision; • [the child's] mental activity and experience are intense; • the child constantly addresses all its capabilities: imagination and mental capacity are in top gear; • obviously enjoys being engrossed in the activity.

© SICS. (Laevers, 2005: 14.)

I have used the manual and 27 video fragments countless times with further education students, undergraduate students and experienced practitioners undertaking refresher or professional development courses. Many thousands of you may also recognise these materials through your own courses, conferences and workshops. What quickly becomes apparent is the ease with which the ideas and approach is assimilated and understood; furthermore, one concurs with Laevers (2000: 25), 'however much involvement may seem to be a subjective property, it is indeed possible to assess the levels of involvement in children and adults in a reliable way'. When considering the video fragments with students, there is always a remarkable consistency in 'levelling judgements'; students are willing to discuss, justify, and use the scales with trust and respect, reflecting Rogoff *et al.*'s (1996: 388) 'learning as a community process of *transformation of participation* in sociocultural activities … not transmission of knowledge from experts or acquisition of knowledge by learners by themselves'. Waters (2009: 25) cites Laevers (2000) reporting 'positively on the inter-observation reliability in studies that have employed the Involvement Scale'.

In September 2014, I collaborated with a landscape architect, Felicity Robinson, in a small church hall based pre-school; the initial impetus for the visit was to assess levels of involvement, particularly outdoors, with a view to looking at where involvement was highest and lowest: the pre-school were planning to move premises and the aim was to be able to design a high quality outdoor environment rather than the 'make-do' of a small strip of tarmac and grass running adjacent to the church hall. Many of you will recognise the challenges of setting up and clearing away such a space outdoors, where the ground levels offer little stimulation and physical space is limited. Focused observations of children using such spaces, however, illuminate rich and playful events and Felicity hoped to use these to plan for a more naturally designed environment. A similar and more lengthy research project has been documented by Learning through Landscapes and by Davy (2013: 226) where 'making changes through practitioner research requires participants to be willing to reflect together on what they have observed, to challenge current practice and assumptions and to be willing to try out new things in direct responses to children's cues'.

Encounter: Joint evaluation of outdoors

Our evaluation of their outside space is that there was no acknowledgement of the outdoors being a different place to be: the equipment and resources were the same as or parallel to those indoors – too much plastic and too much that needed to be put out and put away because of the nature of the materials collected and available. There were no 'loose parts of natural materials'. We acknowledged the limitations of renting a village community space. Felicity will use this 'way of seeing' (using the LIS-YC for the first time) when embarking on landscape design to consider the ingredients of activity level of involvement as well as children's level of involvement in the outdoor environment.

During the first part of the morning, Felicity and I had both focused on one child indoors, to compare our level of involvement score. We watched different episodes of play and came together to discuss our observations. Gardner (2006, in Pound, 2011: 23) 'highlights the importance of reflective practice for *all* professionals'. Pound (ibid. 147) similarly argues: 'pedagogical documentation is fundamentally related to the attempt to see and to understand what happens during the pedagogical experience and seeks to do this without reference to a rigid framework of schema or pre-defined expectations'. The observations were short; narrative snapshots of activity.

> A crucial point about using these scales is that the score is not a judgement on the child but rather on the degree of success of the early years provision in providing the type and quality of experience to enable the child to flourish and achieve deeper level learning. The focus is on the process of learning and the quality of experience for the child rather than the outcome. The numerical indicator on the scale is therefore a message to the early educators themselves as to how 'right' they are getting their provision for that child.
>
> (Davy, 2013: 221–222)

Our score levels were remarkably similar for the child that we observed; we will call him Joseph.

Encounter 1: Joseph paints

Collects apron from basket. Paints with right hand, broad horizontal stripes on green paper pegged to easel. Looks over to floor play. 'I want to build castle.' Interrupts painting to play with child on carpet with A1.★ Outside door opens. He goes out.
   Level 2

Encounter 2: Joseph and the sand kitchen

He moves outside and immediately goes to the sand kitchen with A1. Momentarily looks at resource, leaves, walks to tent and the wobble board, then back to sand kitchen. Brushes sand off hands and uses a spoon to fill a griddle pan and watches parallel child who is playing with A1. Lifts pan. A1 asks if he needs help. He fills bowl and tries to lift griddle pan, which is full of sand.
   Level 2, with elements of 3: 2+

★A1 is a voluntary helper at pre-school.

We can suggest that Joseph has not engaged fully with the observed activities this morning and he frequently moves to different areas of the pre-school. Felicity and I use these observations and those made of another child, Poppy, to compare reliability of using the LIS-YC. We then begin to focus on activities that appear to appeal to children for longer and more intense periods.

Encounter 1: Poppy and the garage

Poppy is on her haunches playing with the three storey plastic garage. She lifts the car to the top storey and watches it run down the slope to the bottom.

 The garage is one of the first floor toys children see as they enter the pre-school. Level 2

Encounter 2: Poppy and the washing line

She looks up from the garage and walks over to the iron, ironing board, brush and pan set. She lies on the floor, brushing it; then examines the toy iron. There is a small rotary washing line. She places all the clothes hangers on the line then holds the peg box, attaching the pegs. She looks up at other children and drops the peg box. Picks up the pegs and looks over at two other children. A3* joins in the play at the rotary line.

 Level 3

Encounter 3: Poppy and the sand kitchen

Poppy has gone outside. She walks to the sand kitchen and chooses a bowl and spoon. A1 clears a space for Poppy to play. She asks A1 a question then shows her a scoop of sand. There is conversation between A1 and Poppy. A1 heard to talk about Poppy's family and home and joining in with role play. Poppy imitates actions and narrative of A1. Poppy empties the kitchen equipment from the box. Watches other three children at the kitchen intensely. Two other children join the play. A1 leaves the area. Poppy continues to pour, giving a spoon to another child and occasionally looks up.

 Level 4

* A3 is a member of staff.

There were two aspects to these brief encounters that began to interest me, beyond that of focusing on the children using LIS-YC/Form 6 (1994) (Observation sheet for the assessment of involvement at the level of an individual child). The first is that the sand kitchen seemed to offer a more stimulating resource to children who played at a more intense level, using imagination, manipulative dexterity, social and language skills. The second was the presence of A1. Earlier in the morning, whilst indoors, my attention had been focused on the sand tray, because of the number of children playing for a lengthy period of time. I began to use LIS-YC/Form 4 (1994) (Observation sheet for the analysis of involvement at the level of an activity).

Encounter: Indoor sand tray

A1 walks to the sand tray. Four children follow. A1 is on her knees playing along-side them. She is actively listening to the children. One child leaves and Jenny momentarily turns her back on the tray to look around the hall. Kayleigh taps her bucket, attempting to make a sand castle. The sand is dry. A1 praises and encourages her. Jenny crouches and looks away from the activity, then leans over sand. A1 is scraping at the bottom of the tray to find objects. Eli joins in and is invited by A1 to come and play. Jenny leaves. Kayleigh has been close to A1 throughout the activity. She stands opposite to A1 across the sand tray and is constantly scooping, digging, crouching and interacting with A1. A1 is digging with a spade and Kayleigh is both busy and watching A1 who is her playmate.

Kayleigh Level 3+; 4 with A1.

My inference here is that the sand tray offers tactile stimulation, imagination and an element of challenge; the interaction with the adult, however, seems to be a significant aspect to Kayleigh's high level of involvement. I make some notes on raising the level of involvement: remove many of the toys (three diggers took a lot of space) from the sand and display them on adjacent area of stage for choosing; use more and damper sand; use stones and shells as objects buried in the sand; alternatively, have spoons and socks for filling sand. I note these for discussion with the staff team at the end of the day.

There were higher levels of play involvement in the sand both indoors and outside.

Encounter: Outdoor sand kitchen

Four children and A1. Eli leaves to play with cars on carpet map. He has already played with cars indoors: interest in movement/forces? Joseph fetches a truck from the floor to go in the sand. A1 is on her knees at children's level. She asks open questions and is encouraging. I see cooking role play by two children. Callum is filling a pan and bowls. 'My pancake is done', says Kayleigh. A1 lifts the curtain to reveal oven.

[I am watching this play with Felicity. We discuss the involvement of the adult, and wonder whether it is her positive intervention or the activity that is holding the children's attention. I ask A1 to quietly leave the activity.]

Callum and Eli continue to play. Kayleigh leaves the sand and runs to A1. 'Don't want to do cooking.' Joseph leaves to play bat and ball. Callum runs with a jug to A1 for some water, which he has asked for previously. A1 returns to sand kitchen.

Reflection: A1 is magnet to children; water butt or access to water would improve area; permanent mud kitchen with access to water at new site. Sand continues to engage generations of children.

It is clear already that many interpretative layers can be found in a brief number of observations over a short period of time. The LIS-YC instrument enables these reflective processes. Laevers (2007a: 22) tells us:

An open framework approach doesn't make any sense if there isn't an environment in which initiatives can be taken, a context that challenges children and offers a myriad of opportunities to be active, explore and create. The richness of the environment can be tested in two ways. Diversity is a first possible entrance. How broad is the horizon of possible experiences? Are all the senses addressed? Are there enough impulses to ensure that each and every developmental domain and disposition is mobilised in children's activities? A second approach brings us to the concept of 'depth'. How much is there to be discovered? Are the activities on offer rich enough to speak to all levels of development of the group of children in the setting? Is the reality brought into the setting complex enough or is it processed by the adult up to the point where the joy of discovery, adventure and serendipity altogether is banned from the daily life of children?

Ulrich and Mayr (in Laevers and Heylen (2003: 33) also state:

> Observing a child's level of involvement during a specific activity does not only tell practitioners about a child's individual interests. When a child does not get involved during a picture book reading session this also may reflect on the way a picture book is being presented.

At the end of the morning I asked the staff team about A1 as she had become a focus of my attention and had high levels of involvement with the children. She had over the past few months offered a rich resource to the pre-school and was soon to undertake a paid position elsewhere. We discussed the high quality of her work and the 'sensitive and empathic awareness of children and an ability to "put themselves in the position of the child"' (Laevers, 1994: 8). McEwan discusses Adult Involvement in Chapter 5.

Using levels of involvement to begin to evaluate provision

As part of our research activity in the pre-school, the staff were interested to use the LIS-YC instrument to add a further layer to the range of assessment already used. They had *heard* of it (but not Laevers) but had not used it. I was able to work together with A2, a member of staff. She suggested we independently observe one of her key children and compare our judgement on level of involvement.

Encounter: Callum and the sand kitchen [Annie]

Callum is standing alongside another child. He looks at child whilst scraping the tray; he is laughing noisily. He fills a bowl and seems aware that A2 is observing. He looks up and smiles. Having filled the bowl, he puts it in the oven, then takes a pan and continues to fill with sand. Once filled, he lifts with both hands and places the pan in the oven.
    Level 4

Encounter: Callum and the sand kitchen [A2]

At the sand tray. He is enjoying mixing the sand while interacting with another child. He fills his bowl with sand and places it in the oven. Looks to see if his bowl of sand is ready, briefly checking behind the oven curtain. Starts filling a frying pan with sand. Allows another child to put sand in his pan and then puts this in the oven as another child puts a pan on top.
    Level 4–5

During our joint reflection, we discussed the differences between levels 4 and 5, using the signals and LIS-YC, and A2's rationale for scoring 5, but that how occasional loss of concentration indicated a closer level to 4. She expressed surprise and pleasure at the level of Callum's social play; he had been extremely distraught at the beginning of the session. She recognised *a different way of seeing*. Burnard *et al.* (2006: 156) cite Arnold (2003) who states: 'Laevers (1997) signals of engagement/involvement may provide appropriate and fertile indicators of the child's learning with the parent and professional.' A2 was excited to be able to share her observation with Callum's parent. This is a very important element of the process. Callum's mum had also been upset when she left him this morning and sharing this observation *with* Callum listening will support his positive experience at pre-school.

Felicity had focused on a spontaneous play opportunity outside, where large templates and chalks were placed near the exit door. A child had asked for water to be able to brush through the template and this had become a busy, involved activity. A2, Felicity and I discussed this activity because of the high levels of involvement (5) and enjoyment. I asked A2 why she thought the activity might have been so engaging. Her response was that it was new. I suggested the messiness, open-ended and risky nature of the activity (risky as in spontaneous, child-led process rather than product) and we discussed how the activity could be extended and re-sited away from the door to a larger area with more water, larger brushes, chalks, paint and pebbles. As Edwards *et al.* (1998: 67) claim: '*What children learn does not follow as an automatic result from what is taught, Rather, it is in large part due to the children's own doing as a consequence of their activities and our resources*' [their italics]. A2 became more and more animated about the possibilities of large pebbles being able to be left outside for children to use creatively. I then talked about water, the sand kitchen and indoor sand tray because the opportunity for community learning presented itself.

The discussion carried on inside and demonstrated very clearly that reflection is as useful, or even more useful, than the observation itself. We talked about the quality interactions of A1, the sand tray possibilities, and which activities had not been played with during our observations. These included the many, many table-top activities and, for example, the three garages on the floor. All staff said that they had not really considered the new age group range of the September cohort, the space they needed, and the different interests they might have. They appeared to enjoy the discussion we were having, acknowledging the challenges of setting up each day, storage and daily routines. Brown, in Chapter 3, discusses further the environmental potential presented through reflection of LIS-YC possibilities. Whalley (2007: 14) explains:

> We shared our understanding of this scale, which is not designed to make judgements about children's performance, but rather as a tool to assess whether the provision that adults are offering to children is sufficiently stimulating to support and extend their learning: 'The child's closely focused attention usually suggests that a good match has been made between an adult's stimulus and some particular or general concern in the child' (Athey, 1990: 63). When a child is 'deeply involved', he or she scores 4–5 on the scale. The provision is appropriate and the pedagogical approach is supportive. When the child is scoring at a low level, there is something wrong with the provision; the adult may be intervening inappropriately or the child's well-being may be low.

We can see, then, that a brief, shared morning of observation using LIS-YC can act as a catalyst for evaluating provision, as well as observing children in a fresh way. Waters (2009: 26) suggests:

> It may be that by considering such initiatives as Carr's (2001) participatory approach to assessment via learning stories and Laevers' concern with attending to 'how children are doing' using involvement scales, we begin to attend to the needs and voices of children within our care in a manner that genuinely places their well-being at the centre of practice.

Experiential education and a curriculum 'fit for purpose'

Having shared Laevers' LIS-YC with a number of experienced practitioners in a sequence of professional development sessions, I was invited to lead some in-service training at a local infant school where a number of student teachers were also undergoing initial training. Both head teacher and deputy head teacher were reviewing their assessment policies and felt that Laevers' ideas 'chime[d] with many other theories, articulating own views of children and education' (Pound, 2011: 84). With a third of children transient in any one school year and an inclusive pedagogy, the school embraced LIS-YC as one of the holistic assessment processes alongside their experiential, project-based curriculum. I was fortunate to be offered a year-long sabbatical as assistant head and foundation stage co-ordinator to further support the developing work of the school. The quality of the care and experience of the children was the most important principle of practice embodied by the staff, perhaps reflecting a key aspect of Laevers' work that he foregrounds and emphasises in many of his research papers and presentations:

> One of the most dramatic implications of the concept of 'deep level learning' has to be situated in the field of educational evaluation. What we have to question is not so much the eagerness (especially by educational authorities) to measure the outcomes of schools. The problem is more that the paradigm dominating these assessments does not take into account the changes that really matter. In the field of communication, for instance, the competence is too much torn up into elementary aspects as vocabulary and grammatical insights. Professionals, including test designers seem to have but a little comprehension of what makes the difference between a poor and highly communicative person.
>
> Changing the way outcomes are measured is only one implication of the 'deep level learning' concept. Another, of course, is the improvement of the quality of education.
>
> Too much education must be discarded as adding 'files' to the system, but not changing the programme' by which incoming stimuli are processed. Real competence is more, and even something else than cleverness. What we want are 'educated' people. If that is the standard, practitioners can limit themselves to one crucial point of reference in the planning and execution of interventions: the involvement of the child.
>
> (Laevers, 2007b: 67–68)

When explaining the experiential approach, Laevers distinguishes between linear – learning from being taught and in a static developmental way – and a more holistic approach; this, the school promoted, 'characterised by the recognition of the dynamic processes beyond what is visible, the interaction between components and participants and the flow or energetic aspects of these interactions' (Laevers, 2007a: 25). Here, the school's pedagogy seemed to be somewhat at odds with current educational policy in England, with desirable goals, core objectives and levels of academic attainment. Laevers (ibid: 18) further points out: 'When we use these insights in relation to educational policy it is not difficult to categorise the educational policy of the eighties and nineties in England as "linear-rational".' A further, lengthy reference will *'chime'* with many early years practitioners:

When we deal with the content of the curriculum, a description in terms of general objectives of the areas of development to be addressed is certainly a sound approach. In the further elaboration, however, some risks have to be faced. The first is related to the tendency to break the general objectives down into a series of operational goals and even relate it to specific age levels. We notice that this kind of elaboration suggests to practitioners (1) that the specific goals cover the whole of a certain developmental areas and (2) that the general objectives in that domain can and must be reached by training the child in each and every separate skill. It certainly gets more risky when policy makers do not leave the implementation of the curriculum open enough and force teachers into all kinds of procedures, such as detailed goal-oriented planning, imposition of specific activities and assessments. The consequence for practice is that a particular educational model is enforced that brings us further away from the advocated 'open framework approach'. The complexity of developmental processes is not taken into account, in particular the fact that children follow diverse routes and that there is a limit to programming deep-level-learning. A developmentally appropriate approach demands active participation of the child who, in his or her response and initiative, will flag what kind of impulse he/she needs at this very moment. Even if it were possible to spell out the developmental stages – I doubt that we already possess that kind of insight for a range of domains – it cannot be taken as a direct guide to set out a detailed route for a group of children. In an alternative, holistic approach, we stress the importance of making sure that the selected developmental domains are described in a way that allows teachers to grasp the essence of it. Holistic doesn't mean 'woolly' or 'esoteric'. It means that the core, the spine, the heart of the matter, when we speak of gross-motor development, social competence, language skills, reasoning is captured. That is exactly what we tried to do in the latest version of the Process-Oriented Child Monitoring System (Laevers, 2005).

(Laevers, 2007a: 26)

Within the first few weeks of entering foundation, our children were observed many times, using learning stories, photographs, post-it comments, shared discussion and through getting to know their parents. Waters (2009: 24) adds:

[Laevers] argues that children experiencing the highest levels of involvement demonstrate their well-being (Anning and Edwards, 2006) and are disposed to engage in 'deep level learning'. (Laevers, 2000: 20). Involvement concerns 'the intensity of the activity, the extent to which one is absorbed' (ibid.) and is linked to Csíkzentmihályi's (1979) 'state of flow' – usually experienced, in young children, in play. (Laevers, 2000).

Meetings between the key workers, SENCO (Special Educational Needs Co-ordinator) and foundation stage co-ordinator resulted in a crude, but usable 'traffic light system' where we aimed to identify those children who had scored low, moderate and high levels of well-being and involvement; our aim was to help our 'red children' to amber and green during the subsequent terms, reflecting that children with low levels would find it difficult to access and enjoy all the experiences on offer and be open to learning opportunities. I had some initial concerns about the label 'red children', but the school having established a 'red curriculum', I was reassured that the label was not used in a prejudicial and discriminative way; the 'red curriculum' was one of the most careful nurturing set of experiences I have encountered in an education setting. The specific needs of each child were discussed and many small group, gentle activities were regularly set up *always* to help to develop children's well-being first; they involved, for example, singing, dancing, stories, puppets, games, working in the garden, dual language play and the sensory room, all activities regularly taking place in larger groups and as informal play experiences. Cuffaro (1995: 1) cites Dewey:

Philosophy is thinking what the known demands of us, what responsive attitude it exacts. It is an idea of what is possible, not a record of accomplished fact. It presents an assignment of something to be done – something to be tried. Its value lies not in furnishing solutions (which can be achieved only in action) but in defining difficulties and suggesting methods for dealing with them. (DE, 326; MW 9: 336)
… it is essential in teaching that practice be grounded in a consciously held, critically examined philosophical framework created by the teacher. [This] represents the choices, values, knowledge, and beliefs of teachers as well as their aspirations, intentions and aims. It serves to guide and inspire and contributes to determining the detail of the everyday life in the classroom.

One child, Ellen, one of the oldest foundation children, had come to school reading and writing fluently; her well-being and involvement scores were low to moderate. She found it difficult to make friends and did not seem to find many activities engaging. The small, nurture groups did not appear to help her. Laevers and Heylen (2003: 183) when analysing Formosinho's research in *Involvement of Children and Teacher Style* state:

[his]qualitative analysis of teachers' thoughts about the use of the involvement scales reveals how this instrument in a self-evident way inspired them to take action. When low levels of involvement are observed, practitioners start to analyse the situation and seek ways to get more intrinsic motivated activity. Where this movement, originally targets the group as a whole, gradually also the individual child gets into focus and specific interventions become part of the teaching.

We watched Ellen carefully, identifying the themes and ideas in her drawing and writing, pairing her up with a younger child who drew, but did not write and encouraged them in book making, then costume making. Alison enjoyed role play, dance and performance and together they presented a formidable and creative team! Sewing was introduced as part of the regular 'making' area and Ellen was also accompanied to a year 1 class for some activities, with a key worker until she felt confident alone.

> During a day in a setting, children go through several types of organization. From an educational point of view it is interesting to describe them in terms of the level of freedom given to the child to make choices between possible activities. On the basis of research in nursery schools, the opportunity for child initiative at the level of class organisation, showed to be one of the most important treatment variables favouring involvement.
>
> (Laevers, 1997: online)

Ellen moved from amber to green in the second term at school. The interventions seemed sufficient to support her well-being so that she was ready to become more deeply involved in new and stimulating learning opportunities.

As a staff group, we were comfortable with using LIS-YC; we used it in conjunction with learning stories and other forms of observational assessment in order to nurture and support children to learn, and to evaluate the learning environment. It was particularly useful for children entering foundation with a history of transience between settings, special needs, home languages *and* those children, like Ellen, who had many, established academic skills already in place. It was *another way of seeing*, and like many settings, we found it a rich resource for discussion and professional development. Like you, we observed as a natural part of early years practice. We used the scales to highlight special concerns and opportunities for individual children; our approach was project based: children's interests were encouraged and resourced. I recall Ellen and Alison able to lead the discussion about our December production; we chose 'When Santa got stuck up the chimney'. Children interested in sewing made the costumes, our 'builders' constructed the chimney after local walks in the school streets to consider chimney design, and we researched reindeer antlers and fairy tales concerning elves.

We also monitored group levels of involvement:

> [it] highlighted the significance of the *enabling context* in the classroom setting and wider school environment. Each of the settings in the study supported the playfulness of teachers and children, and encouraged self-confidence and self-esteem. This supported young children in asking a variety of questions and developing their tendency to learn creatively, through possibility thinking (Burnard *et al.*, 2006). The adults in the settings intentionally valued children's *agency* – that is, children's abilities to have ideas and see these through into actions. They assumed and encouraged children's motivation – which Laevers (1993) and, later, Pascal and Bertram (1997) demonstrated was vital to high engagement as an indicator of quality learning in early childhood education.
>
> (Paige-Smith and Craft, 2008: 99)

Laevers' (2000: 25) research with the LIS-YC has shown that:

the levels of involvement within a setting tend to be more or less stable (Laevers, 1994). They are the result of the interactions between the context (including the way teachers handle their group) and the characteristics of the children. The concepts of well-being and involvement are useful not only for research purposes, but at least as much for practitioners who want to improve the quality of their work.

The essential ingredients to Laevers' work, given in a keynote address (Laevers, 2009) are respect for the child, a positive group climate, a rich environment, teacher style and an open-framework approach. My experiences of working with LIS-YC for a year in an infant school alongside practitioners with whom I was familiar, using Laevers' observational instrument, introducing students to his ideas and being involved in a small-scale project at a pre-school, lead me to suggest that the following points would be helpful: invite 'an experienced other' to support your own professional development; read and discuss first the signals, then the levels as a staff team, using informal knowledge of your children to help illustrate the signs of low, moderate and high levels of involvement; consider the full implications of a shared team pedagogy where an evaluation of the environment and experiential education involving very active learners may well take place; either film children in your setting or work in pairs to observe children, discuss levels of involvement and justify decisions based on signals and confidently carry out further observations; begin to collate individual children's involvement and whole group level involvement; monitor activities with high and low levels of involvement and begin to discuss as a team how you can make changes to activities and environment and the levels of choice available to children. For more information on Laevers' (1994) Ten Action Points, see Chapter 3 by Brown. Lastly, review the steps you are making in connection with any local or national policy initiatives in support of creating effective learning environments.

Laevers (2009), speaking in Scotland, is encouraging:

> To conclude let's bring 'adventure' and 'serendipity' in our settings. Let's give the practitioners confidence so that they can let go of the rigid planning and let's support them to learn to take the perspective of a child and see the gold and seize the golden opportunities that are there.
>
> Well-being and involvement in the child, in the youngsters, in the learner is what we really want. At the same time we know that when we've got that, when the adult is creating that, the adult gets empowered by it. It gives her or him energy. We also know that at team level we need that same quality of well-being and involvement, feeling okay together in a team, but also being entrepreneurial. Having this synergy one plus one is three. Someone has an idea ... another comes in with a new element and adds it. That's where, that's the energy you can sense at a team level. But we all know that is beautiful, well-being, involvement in children, adults and teams, but we are all aware, that's why we are here. But in the end we want that because we hold that important ... most important lever that can shape society for the future.

Provocations

- Evaluate a planned activity to consider how the group reacts and what occurs in the relations between the children? How deeply are they involved? What are the effective ingredients? How comfortable are the children? How stimulated and challenged?
- How experiential is your setting? To what extent do children experience flow, immersion, sense of control and unconscious concentration?
- If you use LIS-YC, how often as a staff group do you *discuss and plan* using individual, group and activity evaluations rather than use them as a record of level outcomes?
- If you have not used LIS-YC, what are your next steps to finding out how you might incorporate this approach into your observational assessment?
- What or whose was the last pebble dropped in your 'pond' and consider the ripple effect.

References

Burnard, P., Craft, A. and Grainger, T. *et al.* (2006). Possibility thinking. *International Journal of Early Years Education*, 14(3): 243–262.

Cuffaro, H. K. (1995) *Experimenting with the World. John Dewey and the Early Childhood Classroom.* New York: Teachers College Press.

Davy, A. (2013) Using Leuven observation and assessment tools to investigate outdoor provision. In Georgeson, J. and Paylor, J. (eds) *International Perspectives on Early Childhood Education and Care.* Maidenhead: Open University Press, Chapter 19.

Edwards, C., Gandini, L. and Forman, G. (eds) (1998) *The Hundred Languages of Children. The Reggio Emilia Approach – Advanced Reflections.* 2nd edn. Westport, CT: Ablex Publishing.

Laevers, F. (ed.) (1994) *The Leuven Involvement Scale for Young Children, LIS-YC.* Manual. Leuven, Belgium: Centre for Experiential Education.

Laevers, F. (1997) Assessing the quality of childcare provision. 'Involvement' as criterion. Available at: http://www.dauphin.be/Microsites%20Algemeen%20DOWNLOADS/CEGO/CEGOeng/pdf/Assesssing%20the%20quality%20of%20childcare%20provision.pdf (accessed 9 September, 2014).

Laevers, F. (2000) Forward to basics! Deep-level learning and the experiential approach. *Early Years*, 20(2): 20–29.

Laevers, F. (ed.) (2005) *Well-being and Involvement in Care Settings. A Process-oriented Self-evaluation Instrument.* Leuven, Belgium: Kind & Gezin and Research Centre for Experiential Education.

Laevers, F. (2007a) The curriculum as means to raise the quality of early childhood education. Implications for policy. *European Early Childhood Education Research Journal*, 13(1): 17–29.

Laevers, F. (2007b) Deep level learning. An exemplary application on the area of physical knowledge. *European Early Childhood Education Research Journal*, 1(1): 53–68.

Laevers, F. (2009) Interview with Ferre Laevers from the Scottish Learning Festival 2009. Available at: http://www.educationscotland.gov.uk/video/f/video_tcm4565868.asp (accessed 14 September, 2014).

Laevers, F. and Heylen, L. (eds) (2003) *Involvement of Children and Teacher Style. Insights from an International Study on Experiential Education. Studia Paedagogica 35.* Leuven, Belgium: Leuven University Press.

Paige-Smith, A. and Craft, A. (eds) (2008) *Developing Reflective Practice in the Early Years.* Maidenhead: Open University Press.

Pound, L. (2011) *Influencing Early Childhood Education. Key Figures, Philosophies and Ideas.* Maidenhead: Open University Press.

Rogoff, B. (1990) *Apprenticeship in Thinking. Cognitive Development in Social Context.* Oxford: Oxford University Press.

Rogoff, B., Matusov, E. and White, C. (1996) Models of teaching and learning. Participation in a community of learners. In Olson, D. and Torrance, N. (eds) *Handbook of Education and Human Development*. Oxford: Blackwell, Chapter 18.

Waters, J. (2009) Well-being. In Waller, T. (ed.) *An Introduction to Early Childhood*. 2nd edn. London: Sage, Chapter 2.

Whalley, M. and the Pen Green Centre Team (2007) *Involving Parents in their Children's Learning*. 2nd edn. London: Sage.

Chapter 3

Involving the environment

Victoria Brown

This chapter considers not just the child's encounters within the physical learning environment and the objects it contains but also the child's interaction with significant people in the environment. It embraces Bruce's (2005: 59) idea that 'the environment is the mechanism by which the Early Childhood Educator brings the child and different aspects of knowledge together' and in line with Bruce's (2005) work aims to consider:

- the child: their stage of development and their interests;
- the socio-cultural context: the values, people, places and things in the physical environment;
- the content: what a child is offered, the learning potential or 'curriculum' in its broadest sense within the learning environment.

This chapter outlines the importance of creating invigorating and captivating environments for children, and with children, which support and nurture both wellbeing and involvement. There is recognition that the learning environment should be viewed as one physical environment, indoors and out, and so this chapter does not concentrate purely on the indoor environment but explores ideas that could be applied equally indoors and outdoors.

It is impossible to consider the physical learning environment as discrete or separate to the emotional environment in a setting. The cultural values on which the setting is based are transmitted in the interactions and exchanges between practitioners, parents and children, and are reflected in the physical environment: the layout, routines and resources. Each setting that values parental partnership will demonstrate their commitment by having a welcoming area in which to meet and greet parents, information boards for parents, and routines and approaches that meet the needs of the families in the setting. Parents will know the names of the practitioners and will feel comfortable approaching them. Practitioners will know something of the home lives and experiences of the children in their care. Equally, areas in the learning environment such as 'den' areas can meet both the physical needs of children – a place to hide, lie down, sleep – and the emotional needs of children – a cosy, safe, defined place with comforting 'home like' furnishings.

It is widely recognised that children need to feel 'at home' (Edgington, 2004: 79), to feel safe, secure and valued within an environment before they can 'branch out' (ibid.: 108) and confidently explore and engage physically, emotionally, socially and cognitively, achieving the ultimate aim of deep level learning and which Csíkszentmihályi

(1990) describes as a 'state of flow'. Schools and settings may represent a very different culture from the one a child is used to (Rogoff, 2003) and so transition into these settings needs to be carefully handled to ensure children settle in smoothly and without stress. This is particularly important in the current educational and political climate with its focus on 'school readiness'. More and more children are entering what can sometimes be quite formal learning environments in schools at increasingly earlier ages, and joining classes where there is already a focus on the achievement of academic results and where regimes of baseline testing are in place. Some children, when first entering a new setting, can tend to stay close to familiar adults or familiar activities and resources. They need time to acclimatise to the new environment and 'find their feet' and their voices. Adults need to recognise this and provide appropriate support and encouragement during this transition period.

The importance of children's wellbeing is therefore fully recognised as central to their learning and development and is the foundation on which the ideas in this chapter are built. This chapter, however, maintains more of a focus on how adults can support the *involvement* of children in the physical learning environment to ensure that children are entering into high quality environments, which meet their holistic needs through a combination of nurturing and loving care and developmentally appropriate education. It takes a holistic view of learning as development and akin to the work of Blenkin and Kelly (1996: 10) considers that 'the prime concern of education should be to develop to the maximum the potential of every child to function as a human being'.

Drawing on the experiences of practitioners, Laevers *et al.* (1997: 7) developed Ten Action Points (Table 3.1) that outline and provide guidance on the adult role in the learning environment.

> Since teachers in pre-school consciously started using involvement and well-being as guidelines for their practice, the development of ideas for an ideal approach received a new impetus. The elaborate know-how you can contribute to well-being and involvement in a concrete manner was given some structure in the so-called 10 points of action. They represent a wide range of ideas which the teacher can draw from: from suggestions for the layout of the classroom to strategies for the guidance of young children with specific developmental needs.

These steps involve the adult in not just observing and listening to children, but in genuinely empathising and deliberately taking on the child's perspective; not just through 'standing in their shoes' but by seeking to understand hearts and minds when planning for and making decisions about the environment. They can also be used as questions for staff self-evaluation and for assessor-visitors to scan the environment to look for signs of quality and effectiveness.

These action steps can be broken down into four main themes, which are considered in turn in this chapter. These themes are:

- the physical environment and resources in the environment;
- the adult role: observing, supporting and enriching play and provision in the environment;
- social and emotional learning opportunities in the environment;
- meeting individual needs within the environment.

Table 3.1 Ten Action Points

I	Rearrange the classroom in appealing corners or areas.
2	Check the content of the corners and replace unattractive materials with more appealing ones.
3	Introduce new and unconventional materials and activities.
4	Observe children, discover their interests and find activities that meet these orientations.
5	Support ongoing activities through stimulating impulses and enriching interventions.
6	Widen the possibilities for free initiative and support them with sound rules and agreements.
7	Explore the relation with each of the children and between children and try to improve it.
8	Introduce activities that help children to explore the world of behaviour, feelings and values.
9	Identify children with emotional problems and work out sustaining interventions.
10	Identify children with developmental needs and work out interventions that engender involvement within the problem area.

Laevers *et al.*, 1997.

The physical learning environment

As Margaret McMillan (cited by Huleatt, 2015: 106) stated 'we are trying to create an environment where education will be almost inevitable'.

The word 'stimulating' is often used to describe learning environments for young children. Colourful mobiles are hung over babies' cots, carpets, toys and display boards may be brightly coloured and children's artwork is often hung from the ceilings and covers the walls. We consider, however, that it is possible for an environment to be overstimulating.

Speech, language and communication needs have been considered a high priority since the Bercow Review (2008). The impact of the environment on these needs had been considered less significant until the Communication Friendly Spaces approach (Jarman, 2007) was introduced. This way of considering the environment includes reflecting on physical aspects such as colour, space, light and temperature. It also considers the impact that spaces can have on emotional security and wellbeing. Large, open plan spaces for young children can be daunting and offer little in the way of security for a young child leaving their carer for the first time. Jarman offers examples of creating smaller contained spaces within a larger environment, using fabrics and cushions to create 'softness' in the environment. She also suggests that the targeted use of colour can reduce overstimulation for young children. Research on young children's views on the use of bright primary colours in classrooms shows that they actually regard this as 'babyish' and do not necessarily choose these colours (Ceppi and Zini, 1998). Ceppi and Zini refer to 'bare' environments with the colour coming from the way the children act upon the environment by, for example, the clothes they wear, the work displayed and the objects they bring into the environment. Further studies highlight the importance of the natural environment to children; 'Children in Reggio' (Bondavalli and Mori, 1993) found children's perspectives included: 'If you are a little sad, you can take a look at the gardens and you'll cheer up' and 'just looking at flowers we get a happy feeling because everything is growing'. Settings in Reggio Emilia often having interconnecting spaces indoors and outdoors, there are windows at child height so the outdoors can be seen indoors. Plants and natural objects may be brought inside to create green spaces and suggest calmness.

Involving children: What kind of spaces do children want?

It is evident that children want spaces that are private and free from adults. Moss and Petrie (2002) suggest that children's need for social interaction with other children and a need to form a social group require spaces that are free from adults. This would suggest that environments should be designed accordingly. Den-making often features in children's play (Tovey, 2005) and can be enhanced by the provision of open-ended resources. It is important to recognise the understanding and confidence needed by practitioners to not be able to see children at all times. This is supported by Clark and Moss (2011) using the Mosaic Approach, a child friendly method of researching with young children, combining informal interviews, cameras, map-making and observations. Their findings indicate that the outdoors, private and social spaces featured highly in photos children took. Another common theme was children valuing personal spaces such as their own peg. Young children also tend to place importance on 'what number they are'. Perhaps numbering pegs with children's ages rather than numbers to 10 or 20 has more significance. This suggests the importance the environment has in fostering a sense of belonging. Other ways to support this include the use of photographs of the children and making links between home and school; for example, having photos of children and their own families in the home corner or having a class bear and book that goes to the home, with space for families to put photos in.

Encounter: Juliet Clark, Robert Mellors Primary and Nursery School in Nottinghamshire

Combining our existing nursery and reception classes in one space was an opportunity to review and rethink our approach to the learning environment. What did our children need? What did our children want? It was just as important for us to have a clear pedagogical underpinning to the environment as it was for us to consider how the children learn phonics most effectively. Speech, language and communication development were high on the agenda, with consideration given to how the environment supports this. We used some of Jarman's (2007) Communication Friendly Spaces approach to influence our decisions about space, colour and stimulation. First, we removed a number of high level displays and replaced these with low level displays, which also acted as partitions between the different areas. The displays were backed with neutral backing and displayed work was kept to display boards to avoid over stimulation. Furniture was used to define areas and create 'cosy' spaces for children to retreat to, either alone or with others. The group rooms, where most adult-led work takes place were designed to enable children to listen and attend, many distractions were removed. Softness was added, created with soft furnishings and drapes.

We considered the presentation of resources, reflecting on how to best attract children to particular experiences. Aesthetically it was important to use the highest quality of resources and present them in a way that choices could be made easily. Reducing the amount on offer also helped the children to make choices without being overwhelmed. The move towards children selecting their own resources and having choice has in some settings led to too much choice. Fewer, good quality buckets and spades displayed attractively so the size can be seen and compared, is preferable to ten buckets stacked up.

Listening to Children: In order to gain the children's views about their environment, a variety of methods were used, including using photographs, map-making and informal interviews, These are aspects of the Mosaic Approach (Clark and Moss, 2011), which when pieced together enable a rich picture of children's views and opinions to be compiled. The children became involved in planning of two areas: the home corner and an outside 'cosy area'. This resulted from findings that indicated the home corner was a favourite area but was too noisy and too small, and that there were no quiet spaces outside.

It could be argued that involving children in decisions about their environment has an impact on levels of involvement. They develop a sense of ownership of the areas, which can lead to children taking a high degree of pride and care with their environment through keeping it tidy and suggesting improvements. In fact, the act of involving children itself is a real-life experience that offers lots of opportunities for writing, reading and calculating for a purpose. Sobel (2002: 61 sums this up: 'If we allow children to shape their own world in childhood, they will grow up knowing and feeling that they can participate in shaping the big world.'

Real resources

Resources that are low in cost but that afford opportunities for high levels of involvement often yield more creative and exploratory play than more costly resources, as was evidenced by the preschool research in Chapter 2. The preschools and infant toddler centres in the municipality of Reggio Emilia in Northern Italy make good use of the Remida centre, where there is an abundance of recycled materials and objects waiting to be reimagined and re-created through open-ended play. The name Remida comes from the legend of King Midas. Objects that are broken or unused can be given a new life or 'turned into gold' with a little imagination.

Real objects offer an authenticity to children. They know the difference between real and pretend. Using real food such as packets, tins and dried pasta or lentils enables children to engage with items they may have experience of from home, or following a cooking experience. Real items such as kettles, utensils and saucepans allow children to experience natural materials that offer a different sensory experience to using plastic (Bruce, 2005).

Natural and open-ended resources enable more creativity to take place as they can be used in many different ways. Nicholson's (1971: 6) theory of loose parts suggests that features that are moveable and malleable are more open-ended and can be combined in many different ways and therefore have more play potential. 'In any environment, both the degree of inventiveness and creativity, and the possibility of discovery, are directly proportional to the number and kind of variables in it.'

Loose parts and everyday materials may be used in discovery or heuristic play and may include found objects, recycled, manufactured and natural objects. Materials with heuristic play potential include: sponges, pan lids, pebbles, pine cones, keys, woollen balls, chains. Their use is not predetermined by practitioners but open to the child's innovation and imagination and therefore play becomes limitless in scope and generally more involved. Objects can be grasped, squeezed and explored through rolling, banging or shaking, can be placed and rearranged, their texture, weight and properties investigated by touch and action. Materials are often attractively presented to babies and young children in treasure baskets, or 'concept' boxes (for example, collections of shiny objects) and provide a rich sensory and exploratory experience for children enabling them to make sense of their world and how things work (Goldschmeid and Jackson, 1994).

Fundamental to the discussion about environments is the idea that what is provided by adults in planning the learning environment, and where and how it is presented, has the potential to influence, extend and support the type of learning that takes place.

Observing, supporting and enriching play and provision in the environment

Action points 4, 5 and 6 (Laevers et al., 1997) consider how adults can act in the learning environment to observe, support and challenge children in their play and activities in order to support their involvement and deep level learning. Children do not always require an adult's presence to achieve deep involvement and meaning from their play but an adult needs to be alert to the child's needs so that they are on hand to offer support if necessary, as a resource for children. Katz (1993) sees the importance of the adult role as being there as a resource for children. Children are social beings, and learn within social contexts; therefore an enriched environment without meaningful interactions with interested others, companions in inquiry and co-adventurers in play seems to be of limited value. Whilst the acceptance and involvement of an adult in children's play can be seen as a contentious issue, which we explore later in the chapter, Duffy (2006: 118) cites the work of Kinder who observed that the physical presence of an adult and their involvement in activities increased participation, concentration and exploration in children.

Laevers (2006) believes that when children are deeply involved in an activity they are displaying sustained concentration and are operating at the very edges of their capabilities. The knowledgeable practitioner is able to work as a facilitator enabling children to get the most out of the learning environment; Vygostsky (1978: 90) describes this as supporting the child as they work at the limits of their independent capabilities and proposes that

> an essential feature of learning is that it creates the zone of proximal development; that is, learning awakens a variety of internal developmental processes that are able to operate only when the child is interacting with people in his environment and in cooperation with his peers. Once these processes are internalized, they become part of the child's independent developmental achievement.

Gripton, in the final chapter of this book, explores assessment and planning in greater detail.

Responding to children's interests

Why children's interests? The influence of Reggio Emilia can be seen in the adult role in provoking and responding to children's emerging questions and curiosities (Rich et al., 2006), which can act as catalysts for exploring possibilities (Gripton, 2013) and which requires the teacher to respond to the possibilities revealed through play (Craft, 2011). If practitioners stick to pre-determined topics or themes, then learning experiences for children can seem contrived, as experiences are made to fit the theme rather than the child (Bruce, 2005). Instead, if practitioners observe children and note their interests then 'mini themes' will emerge that are meaningful to children. Laevers demonstrates how this reaction from adults to children's interests fosters and promotes high involvement; for example, observing a group of children racing cars down guttering could lead to the provision of car-themed reading books and material, numbered racing tracks, different surfaces, posters of cars, manuals and driving licences, which would all lead to higher involvement levels than a generic topic on transport. This way of responding to children's interests also seems to have an impact on boys' particular styles of learning. It is possible that some topics lend themselves more to the interests of boys or girls, and practitioners should ensure that areas of interest are adapted so that they appeal to everyone. Working on several mini themes at once means that several interests can be catered for, thereby offering a more inclusive environment. Certainly, it has been widely cited (Paley, 1986; Edwards *et al.*, 1998) that many boys prefer to engage in more active learning, and the outdoors lends itself particularly well to this type of learning; this is considered in greater detail in Moran's chapter, which follows. Practitioners should, however, consider whether they value learning outdoors as much as they value learning indoors; for example, if a child has engaged with writing outside, making a label for a large-scale building or writing labels for plants, is it necessary to insist that they also write indoors? Practitioners should also consider where they place themselves in the physical environment, as this may show where their values lie. If a practitioner always bases themselves at focus activities at a 'work table' then the children may get the message that their play is not valued. Consideration needs also to be given to the physical space in which activities occur; focus or 'work' type activities always taking place at tables rather than in other areas of the environment indoors or outdoors also presents a hidden curriculum.

Marsh and Millard (2000) suggest that we need to provide what children are really interested in to avoid and/or offer what we consider culturally or educationally acceptable. In the following example a setting is facing a dilemma:

Encounter: Community culture

In very close proximity to the setting is a fast food restaurant and takeaway, part of a global chain. This is extremely popular with the children, many of whom have parties there. A parent manages this local franchise and offers the setting packaging and merchandise, which would allow them to provide this as a play area for their children. On the one hand, this would be popular with the children but on the other, considerations such as protecting children from advertising aimed directly at them, promoting healthy eating and environmental concerns make this controversial.

The setting could embrace the play as a fun learning opportunity or avoid the play and the subject entirely; it could also create the fast food play area and use it as an opportunity to educate and discuss the issues. In this case after discussion with parents the setting chose the latter and reported high levels of involvement not just in the role play but in discussion around the issue of litter being thrown into the grounds; as a result the children successfully petitioned for recycling bins to be installed in the car park and designed posters, which the restaurant agreed to display asking customers to carefully consider where they disposed of their rubbish after eating.

Wood (2007), however, cautions against basing a curriculum on children's interests as these interests may be transitory and may privilege the play of the dominant children in the group; instead she proposes that practitioners concentrate on supporting children in making rich and meaningful connections in their play so that they are able to link play themes to their own experiences and find their own meanings.

To fully embrace children's interests we need to know about their home experiences; these are part of who the children are and we should not separate or ignore home and school interests. Involving children and families in planning can lead to the discovery of rich play themes that are authentically based around children's interests and fascinations. We need to bring home experiences into the classroom, provide opportunities for children to talk about their experiences out of the setting, and to bring in objects and photographs from home to display. Equally we need to be able to share school or setting experiences in a rich dialogue with home. This kind of exchange occurs in the following encounter from Moran and Brown (2013). Here we meet Ed who is deeply involved in his play with the train track over the course of a week.

Encounter: Ed and his trains

Ed is playing with the train set. He has been playing with this all week, linking bridges together. By Friday he is trying to elevate the track, building it up on wooden bricks. He works with focus and determination, persisting in the face of difficulty and instability. He uses gesture to communicate what he is trying to build … a bridge, we think. At home time photographs are shared and mum exclaims 'that's the Ribblehead viaduct! We went there at half term. He loved it'. A meaning is shared, an adventure begins …

Action Step 4. Observe children, discover their interests and find activities that meet these orientations.

Action Step 5. Support ongoing activities through stimulating impulses and enriching interventions.

Ed is undoubtedly displaying what Laevers (2006: 5) describes as 'intense mental activity'. His preoccupation and fascinations were noticed and recognised and sensitively supported by the practitioners in his setting: they provided small bricks, conversation and moral support as he tried to build stairs up to the platform. Bruce (2005) sums up the role played by adults in encounters such as these in three keywords: observe, support, extend; however it is easy to see such play as repetitive and lacking in challenge and requiring adult intervention in order to refocus and widen the child's interests. For this child there seemed to be a real emotional connection and drive to understand his experience and the wider world through his play.

Time

Edgington (2004) writes passionately about the need for practitioners to provide sufficient time for children to explore, engage and become involved in their play and the experiences on offer in the environment. Time needs to be used flexibly to enable children to pursue their interests and agendas at length and in depth. Spending a sustained period of time in a rich learning environment enables children to consolidate skills and concepts, and make links in their learning across the curriculum and across learning environments inside and outdoors. It can increase both motivation and concentration. The practitioners in the above encounter gave Ed the precious gift of time and space to deeply explore his fascination and play agenda for as long as he needed, ultimately allowing him to recreate, communicate and make meaning from his experiences. This flow of activity over time is important; Laevers (2006: 6) states 'any disturbance or interruption would be experienced as a frustrating rupture of a smoothly running activity' and could prematurely curtail a unique learning opportunity.

In the following extract from an interview with a practitioner in a large Foundation Stage unit we see how the needs of children are balanced against the needs of the setting.

Encounter: Free flow play

We have free flow child-initiated play indoors and outdoors, we try and give them an extended block. We have areas of continuous provision such as sand, water, creative areas and role play. Children have free rein over the environment and can go back to the same thing repeatedly. We leave name labels out and they have a 'work in progress area'. Children initiate their own projects. They have been measuring lengths of wool recently and wrapping them in their hair. Children can come to assembly dressed up or with wool in their hair. We don't want to stop the play if we can avoid it. We need to think carefully before we call a child away from their play to come and read. Whose needs are more important, ours or the child's?

This demonstrates the need to provide an environment that provides a sense of security; where children know their projects can be returned to, models can be built on the next day, pictures can be finished, play agendas continued or expanded. It also requires an environment where routines such as playtimes, snack times and assemblies do not interrupt the flow of the play. Many settings utilise a 'snack bar' approach that operates in an ongoing way during the session, where children can access food when they feel hungry. These can still be nurturing and sociable times where children interact with their friends and interested adults as they eat. Equally many settings adopt free flow play between indoors and outdoors rather than adhering to set indoor and outdoor times. Both are good examples of practice that flows with the needs, interests and involvement of the child.

Interacting in and extending play

Play matters to children; it is a context that deeply absorbs and actively involves them, and the environment should be organised to privilege this involvement. The freedom inherent in child-initiated play is a central pillar of the work of Laevers and settings that serve the 0–5 age range. In Laevers' experiential educational settings children are able to choose from a rich range of activities for 65 per cent of the available time. This activity enables children's initiative and exploratory drive and provides intrinsically motivating and rewarding activity, which Laevers argues results in episodes of intense involvement (Laevers, 2006). Ensuring all children have equal status and power in their independent and autonomous free play is an issue all practitioners need to explore in order to ensure inclusion and equality of opportunity within their play environments.

It is important to consider how much freedom should be offered in settings for children to experience quality play. Moyles and Worthington (2011) found that teacher beliefs about the open-ended nature of play were not upheld in practice owing to pressures from curriculum changes, and an instrumental view of assessment. They suggest there is a limited amount of time for play in reception classes and note the lack of quality and creativity of this play. It would appear that some practitioners, whilst convinced of the benefits, are unsure of how to plan to include play within their daily provision whilst remaining compliant with the perceived demands of Ofsted, assessment and curriculum (Moyles, 2010). They may also lack confidence in articulating their beliefs about the educational value of play (Moyles, 2010; Williams, 2010) and lack depth of understanding of how to incorporate interactive pedagogies into their teaching (Stephen, 2010). Both McInnes et al. (2011) and Walsh et al. (2011) argue that this may result in mistrust of the educational value of play activities and a reluctance to give choice and control to children. McInnes et al. (2011) identified two main constraints on practice in foundation stage settings; lack of time to prepare play experiences in the environment and the pressure for more teacher-led activity as the year progressed.

In recent years the notion of adult and child being jointly involved in the co-construction of learning has become popular and has led to a reconceptualisation of play in terms of *playful structure* (Walsh et al., 2011) or *playful pedagogies* (Moyles, 2010) with practitioners adopting a range of integrated pedagogies in their work with children (Wood, 2013), acting as co-players and bringing playfulness to their teaching and interactions.

Hadley (2002), drawing on Csíkszentmihályi's (1990) theory of flow, discusses the positioning of adults as being either outside or inside the process of children's play and asserts both as part of the practitioner's repertoire; however, in practice, being accepted inside the flow of a child's play as an adult can sometimes be problematic owing to the conflicting agendas of the practitioner and the child. In the following extract we see the tension between the different purposes of adults and children in the setting.

Encounter: Playing on bikes

Focus activities can be playful and are often adult-led and are more like focused exploring together with the children. Nurture groups are also used to develop confidence, social skills or language skills depending on the needs of the children. It is difficult as you are taking children away from their play and it doesn't feel valuing.

And then there is the child who needs to be in all those groups and they don't get the chance to do the thing they need most – which is play! Children tend to spend a lot of time outside, on the bikes, in the mud. We need to consider how to get them to engage in maths for example but without taking the bikes or the mud away. It wouldn't be valuing to place higher status on the maths learning we want them to do over their play.

Here the practitioner notes the difficulty in meeting the needs of all in the setting. Hedges (2010) highlights what can be seen as an uncomfortable relationship between learning through play, and teaching through play, raising the question of whose goals and interests are privileged: the teacher's or the child's? Wood (2011) considers the ethics of adult involvement in children's play as contentious. Play is a realm where traditionally children rule yet adults may seek to assert their control by harnessing play to learning objectives in order to meet children's perceived needs as defined by curricular and school agendas. Children use and should be free to use the freedom inherent in play situations to establish their own identities, agency and power. Nolan and Kilderry (2010) note the power held by adults as they determine the nature of children's 'needs' and express concern that this perpetuates the idea that teacher 'knows best'. Practitioners need to be aware of the position of power they hold and use this respectfully, at times relinquishing control despite external pressures on them from parents and the curriculum, in order for children to have 'a genuine stake in how things are done and in what may be learned' (Rose and Rogers, 2012: 70).

It is therefore essential that practitioners consider how they communicate and interact with children, the ways in which they engage with, offer and guide activities in the environment, as these all influence how children perceive and respond to the activity. Laevers (2006: 8) describes stimulating interventions by adults as '*open impulses that engender a chain of actions in children*'; these interactions are seen as crucial in making the difference between children's level of involvement with an activity. Laevers and Moons (1997) suggest that episodes of joint interaction can be divided into 'Action stimulating', 'Communication stimulating' and 'Thought stimulating' exchanges.

In the following encounter taken from Brown (2014) we meet a trainee teacher striving to engage with a child in a reception class in a structured play activity with limited success owing to her concern with achieving the prescribed learning outcome.

Encounter: The spider

The children have been asked to use the play dough to make a mini beast that is the same on both sides. The child has made a model that has eight legs on the bottom and two legs on the top; she says, 'It is a spider'. The trainee sitting across the corner of the table looks at this and says 'mmm how many legs does a spider have? … How many legs have you got on the bottom? … And how many have you got on the top? … Why don't you count them?' The child looks at the model and counts as she has been asked. The trainee continues … 'is your model the same on both

(Continued)

(Continued)

sides?' The child looks again at her model and replies 'yes'. The trainee tries again, 'If you have more legs on the bottom … how can it be the same? A spider has the same number of legs on each side of its body.' The child looks at the trainee, picks up a ruler and uses the ruler to draw a vertical line through the mini beast – she turns the dough mat towards the trainee teacher. It is now apparent that the spider has four legs on each side of the ruler at the bottom. The child says 'those are two antennae at the top, not legs'.

Action Step 5. Support ongoing activities through stimulating impulses and enriching interventions

We can see the quite different perspectives taken during the interaction between the trainee and an increasingly exasperated child. Sometimes, as in this extract, with the best of intentions, when we feel we are providing action, communication or thought stimulating impulses we can instead bombard the child with too many questions, allow minimal time for their response, or fail to genuinely listen to a child because of our own preconceptions and motives. The trainee herself recognised the task was too prescribed and that her expectation was based on the accuracy of the final product more than the learning process. It serves to show us that sometimes it is what we do not say that is most powerful, the spaces we provide for thinking time, the raised eyebrow, the gesture, the openness of a task. When an adult asks too many questions, they are holding too much power and direction for the interaction to be considered as a genuine shared dialogue. In many cases the offering of a comment instead of a question may be more effective as a strategy to support sustained shared thinking and models the process of externalising internal thought processes, which children may naturally do in their 'pole-bridging talk'. Hanen (2011) considers that 'owling', where the adult must *Observe, Wait and Listen* is a useful strategy that adults can use to support genuinely open forms of dialogue.

Social and emotional learning

Action points 7 and 8 consider the affective and existential domain of emotions, feelings, behaviour, relationships and values. These are commonly explored in a structured way in many settings through circle time activities or as part of routines in the day, for example, noting which children have been good helpers and the reasons why, or children choosing a symbol, colour or fabric to represent their mood on entering the setting that day or through the use of persona dolls. In order to fully meet children's social and emotional learning needs we need to explore the world of feelings and emotions beyond circle times. Some settings have adapted their physical spaces to incorporate 'nurture spaces', calming places where children can 'just be'. Children are invited to use the space as a positive time out place (Nelsen *et al.*, 2007), a safe place where they can experience, learn to soothe themselves and begin to regulate their own emotions and behaviour.

The environment should be considered as a whole; not just the physical environment but the social and emotional atmosphere created in the setting. In a positive emotional environment adults will be respectful of children and of each other and the families who attend the setting. Staff will model the behaviours, attitudes and values they wish to see in their everyday encounters. We should aim to create a space where everyone, whether they are a member of staff, a child or a parent, feels safe to question, explore, and express their thoughts, feelings and ideas. In this way children and families will feel from their first contact that this is a place where they feel known, accepted and belong. This first contact with a setting is powerful; Huleatt (2015) describes how parents make up their mind about a setting in the first five minutes of their visit, using their instinct to ascertain whether they feel welcome and whether they think their child will be happy in the setting. If we are to sustain a family's contact with the setting in the long term, it is vital that relationships get off on the right footing from the very beginning, as is further explored in Chapter 6. If we manage to earn and build the respect and trust of a family in the first stages of education the positive relationship is more likely to be sustained throughout the contact with the setting or school.

We also need to build the respect and trust of children and between children. In the following encounter we find a setting experiencing a crisis in developing their own social and emotional climate as they balance the rights of children to play unhindered against the need for structure, safety and order. The setting is working with a local authority consultant on developing a positive environment for behaviour that builds on their beliefs about autonomy and choice.

Encounter: With a preschool

A preschool pride themselves on their provision for free play. It is indeed wonderful; children are free to make, create, explore, decide where to play, who to play with and for how long. Resources are well chosen and entice them to go deeper into their play. Adults observe and provide resources but rarely interact as they do not wish to interfere. There are no real rules or boundaries, this is most noticeable at tidy time where children decide that they do not wish to help and in fact throw objects around the setting, occasionally bouncing off other children. 'What can we do?' the practitioners shrug. With the help of some video footage the staff are supported to unpick the daily experience of the children and begin to understand that although there is freedom and ownership, there is a distinct lack of respect and no real sense of community in the setting. The practitioners decide to show the video to the children in small groups and ask them their thoughts. 'We weren't being kind were we?' 'Ow, that hurt me.' 'We were hiding and not tidying.' Children began to volunteer what they could do differently: 'We should all help to tidy shouldn't we?' With a few simple tweaks the setting begins to transform itself. Children have a meeting time at the beginning and end of the day, just for a few minutes, a sociable time to build relationships, talk about the day, sing, share and begin to establish a few positive rules.

Action points:

7   Explore the relation with each of the children and between children and try to improve it.
8   Introduce activities that help children to explore the world of behaviour, feelings and values.

The negotiation that occurs in this encounter is led by the children's own thoughts and ideas. It amply demonstrates that given the chance, children can demonstrate they are capable thinkers, powerful problem solvers and have the capacity to be responsible citizens. Katz (1993) describes such children as having positive learning dispositions; they are co-operative, creative, resourceful, inventive and empathic. These dispositions are acquired, supported, or weakened by experiences in a learning environment though interaction with significant adults and peers (Bertram and Pascal, 2002). In settings that are concerned to foster positive learning dispositions, children will be encouraged to persist, supported to take a risk and to try out their own ideas, and undesirable behaviours such as intolerance, or selfishness will be discouraged. Dweck and Leggett (1988) describe such children as having a mastery orientation. These children will have an inner 'I can' script and be more resilient, independent and self-motivated. They are more likely to see learning as a process where it is okay to make mistakes, 'because I am still learning', or 'I just need to keep practising and then I will be able to do it'.

Meeting individual need

Action points 9 and 10 relate to giving individual attention to and providing provision for children with individual needs. Laevers describes these as 'children with special developmental needs' (2013: 5). I would argue the perspective should be broadened to consider children's cultural, linguistic, physical, behavioural, social and emotional needs as well as their cognitive development needs. Wherever children are exhibiting signs of low involvement or wellbeing there is a need for some form of individual attention; they could be offered adult or peer support and adaptations could be made to the physical space, resources or routines. Laevers (2013: 8) states:

> ... one starts where one stands, with the room, the children, the material, the methods and all the limitations linked to the actual situation. Then a field of action is chosen and initiatives are taken that have the potential to bring about an increase in wellbeing and/or involvement. This increase – how small it may be – is experienced as a success and drives one towards new initiatives.

It is important to provide inclusive learning environments that embrace the diversity of the setting and local community. Communities are increasingly characterised by cultural and linguistic diversity and many settings have children from a variety of multicultural backgrounds that encompass different values, practices and traditions (Ang, 2010). Culture is a complex matter, it is easy to assume the needs of a particular cultural group. Of course, in reality, there can be just as much cultural variation within cultures as between cultures. As practitioners then, working with parents, families and communities to discuss their needs is vital. It also requires reflective practice by practitioners in order to confront pre-given images and to avoid over-generalising and stereotyping of different cultural groups (Siraj-Blatchford, 2006). Lindon (2015) notes the importance of children seeing positive images of themselves and their families reflected in the play resources, images and books within the environment. It is equally important to develop and extend children's understanding of diversity 'beyond their own backyard' (Lindon, 2015: 1) and a rich range of creative play materials and experiences offer children a chance to step into the lives of others outside their immediate family (Duffy, 2006).

We must remember to consider all children as unique learners, whoever they are, wherever they are from and wherever they are on the continuum of learning and development; children who are at emergent levels through to those identified as 'gifted and able'. All children need an appropriate level of challenge and risk in their environment; this can be considered with reference to Csíkszentmihályi's concept of *flow*, an ideal state occurring where there is a high level of perceived challenge in a task or play activity matched with a high level of skill in the child. All children need to be appropriately challenged in their learning no matter their level of development, otherwise play is in danger of becoming routine and repetitive. Practitioners, therefore, through conversation and observation of children need to become aware of individual children's interests and motivations, the questions they are asking of objects or themselves: '*What is this?*' '*What can it do?*' '*What can I do with it?*' in order to support the child most effectively in their learning.

Provocations

- In the preschools and infant toddler centres in Reggio Emilia, the learning environments are designed to represent the values held by the practitioners. Mirrors are used to represent reflective practice and to demonstrate that multiple perspectives exist, and spaces are interconnected to demonstrate the importance of social relationships and connectedness to the community and outdoors. Does your environment represent your values? Try and look at it from the view of a parent entering your setting. What is the first thing they see? Get down to the child's height and see what it looks and feels like from their perspective. What does it look like is valued here?
- Is your setting noticeably absent of clutter? Are there calm and quiet spaces? What elements of the setting give it a distinctive colour or focus? Is your environment a space for being 'cosy' together in?
- Do you have an abundance of open-ended or natural materials or is your setting characterised by predominantly plastic resources with set uses?
- Which areas are valued by children? Do you know which areas are used well? Is the environment and the resources it contains reviewed on a daily basis and adapted accordingly?
- Do displays represent your work or children's work? If a new child or family were entering your setting, would they find familiar cultural objects, would their language be represented? Are a variety of images and family structures conveyed? Do some areas appeal more to girls or boys?

References

Ang, L. (2010) Critical perspectives on cultural diversity in early childhood. Building an inclusive curriculum and provision. *Early Years*, 30(1): 41–53.

Bercow, J. (2008) *The Bercow Report. A Review of Services for Children and Young People (0–19) with Speech, Language and Communication Needs*. Nottingham: Department for Children, Schools and Families (DCSF).

Bertram, T. and Pascal, C. (2002) What counts in early learning. In Saracho, O. N. and Spodek, B. (eds) *Contemporary Perspectives in Early Childhood Curriculum*. Greenwich, CT: Information Age, pp. 241–256.

Blenkin, G. and Kelly, A. V. (1996) *Early Childhood Education. A Developmental Curriculum.* 2nd edn. London: PCP.

Bondavalli, M. and Mori, M. (1993) Children in Reggio Emilia look at their school. *Children's Environments,* 10(2): 39–45.

Brown, V. (2014) Sustained shared conversations. In Woods, A. (ed.) *The Characteristics of Effective Learning. Creating and Capturing the Possibilities in the Early Years.* London: Routledge.

Bruce, T. (2005) *Early Childhood Education.* London: Hodder Arnold.

Ceppi, G. and Zini, M. (eds) (1998) *Children's Spaces and Relations. Metaproject for the Environment of Young Children.* Reggio Emilia: Domus Academy Research Centre/Reggio Children.

Clark, A. and Moss, P. (2011) *Listening to Young Children. The Mosaic Approach.* 2nd edn. London: National Children's Bureau.

Craft, A. (2011) Creativity and early years settings. In Paige-Smith, A. and Craft, A. (eds) *Developing Reflective Practice in the Early Years.* 2nd edn. Maidenhead: Open University Press, pp. 87–100.

Csíkszentmihályi, M. (1990) *Flow. The Psychology of Optimal Experience.* New York: HarperCollins.

Duffy, B. (2006) *Supporting Creativity and Imagination in the Early Years.* 2nd edn. Maidenhead: Open University Press.

Dweck, C. S. and Leggett, E. (1988) A social cognitive approach to motivation and personality. *Psychological Review,* 95(2): 256–273.

Edgington, M. (2004) *The Foundation Stage Teacher in Action.* London: PCP.

Edwards, C., Gandini, L. and Forman, G. (eds) (1998) *The Hundred Languages of Children. The Reggio Emilia Approach – Advanced Reflections.* 2nd edn. Westport, CT: Ablex Publishing.

Goldschmeid, E. and Jackson, S. (1994) *People under Three.* London: Routledge.

Gripton, C. (2013) Planning for endless possibilities. In Woods, A. (ed.) *Child-initiated Play and Learning: Planning for Possibilities in the Early Years.* London: Routledge, pp. 8–22.

Hadley, E. (2002) Playful disruptions. *Early Years,* 22(1): 9–17.

Hanen (2011) *Owl to Let your Child Lead.* Hanen Early Language Program. Available at: http://www.hanen. org/Images-for-public-site/Links---Sample-PDFs/ITTTp17-18S.aspx (accessed 18 January, 2014).

Hedges, H. (2010) Whose goals and interests? The interface of children's play and teachers' pedagogical practices. In Brooker, L. and Edwards, S. (eds) *Engaging Play.* Maidenhead: Open University Press, pp. 25–39.

Huleatt, H. (2015) The indoor environment at work. In Hays, S. (ed.) *Early Years Education and Care. New Issues for Practice from Research.* London: Routledge, pp. 105–126.

Jarman, E. (2007*) Communication Friendly Spaces. Improving Speaking and Listening Skills in the Early Years Foundation Stage.* Nottingham: Basic Skills Agency.

Katz, L. G. (1993) *Dispositions. Definitions and Implications for Early Childhood Practices.* Catalogue No. 211 Perspectives from ERIC/EECE: Monograph series no. 4.

Laevers, F. (2006) *Making Care and Education More Effective Through Wellbeing and Involvement. An Introduction to Experiential Education.* Belgium: Leuven Institute.

Laevers, F. (2013) Making care and education more effective through wellbeing and involvement. An introduction to Experiential Education. Conference paper given at Pen Green Research Centre, Corby, UK, March 2013.

Laevers, F., Bogaerts, M. and Moons, J. (1997) *Enhancing Wellbeing and Involvement in Children. An Introduction in the Ten Action Points.* Video. Leuven, Belgium: Centre for Experiential Education.

Lindon, J. (2015) Cultural diversity in the early years. Community playthings. Available at: http:// www.communityplaythings.co.uk/learning-library/articles/cultural-diversity-in-the-early-years (accessed 18 June, 2015).

McInnes, K., Howard, J., Miles, G. and Crowley, K. (2011) Differences in practitioners' understanding of play and how this influences pedagogy and children's perceptions of play. *Early Years,* 31(2): 121–133.

Marsh, J. and Millard, E. (2000) *Literacy and Popular Culture. Using Children's Culture in the Classroom.* London: PCP.

Moran, M. and Brown, V. (2013) Play as a space for possibilities. In Woods, A. (ed.) *Child-initiated Play and Learning. Planning for Possibilities in the Early Years*. London: Routledge, pp. 83–95.

Moss, P. and Petrie, P. (2002*) From Children's Services to Children's Spaces. Public Policy, Children and Childhood*. London: Routledge Falmer.

Moyles, J., (2010) Practitioner reflection on play and playful pedagogies. In Moyles, J. (ed.) *Thinking about Play*. Maidenhead: Open University Press, pp. 13–30.

Moyles, J. and Worthington, M. (2011) *The Early Years Foundation Stage Through the Daily Experiences of Children*. TACTYC Occasional Paper No. 1. Association for the Professional Development of Early Years Educators

Nelsen, J., Erwin, C. and Duffy, R. A. (2007) *Positive Discipline for Preschoolers*. New York: Three Rivers.

Nicholson, S. (1971) How not to cheat children. The theory of loose parts. *Landscape Architecture*, 62: 30–35.

Nolan, A. and Kilderry, A. (2010) Postdevelopmentalism and professional learning. Implications for understanding the relationship between play and pedagogy. In Brooker, L. and Edwards, S. (eds) *Engaging Play*. Maidenhead: Open University Press, pp. 108–122.

Paley, V. G. (1986) *Boys and Girls. Superheroes in the Doll Corner*. Chicago: University of Chicago Press.

Rich, D., Casanova, D., Dixon, A., Drummond, M. J., Durrant, A. and Myer, C. (2006) *First Hand Experience. What Matters to Children*. Ipswich: Rich Learning Opportunities.

Rogoff, B. (2003) *The Cultural Nature of Human Development*. Oxford. Oxford University Press.

Rose, J. and Rogers, S. (2012) *The Role of the Adult in Early Years Settings*. Maidenhead: Open University Press.

Siraj-Blatchford, I. (2006) Educational disadvantage in the early years: How do we overcome it? Some lessons from research. *European Early Childhood Education Research Journal*, 12(2): 5–20.

Sobel, D. (2002) *Children's Special Places. Exploring the Role of Dens, Forts and Bush Houses in Middle Childhood*. Detroit, MI: Wayne State University.

Stephen, C., (2010) Pedagogy. The silent partner in early years learning. *Early Years*, 30(1): 15–28.

Tovey, H. (2005) *Playing Outdoors. Spaces and Places, Risks and Challenge*. Maidenhead: Open University Press.

Vygotsky, L. S. (1978) *Mind in Society*. Cambridge. MA: Harvard University Press.

Walsh, G., Sproule, L., McGuinness, C. and Trew, K. (2011) Playful structure. A novel image of early years pedagogy for primary school classrooms. *Early Years*, 32(2): 107–119.

Williams, B. (2010) Reflecting on child initiated play. In Moyles, J. (ed.) *Thinking about Play*. Maidenhead: Open University Press, pp. 81–100.

Wood, E. (2007) Reconceptualising child-centred education. Contemporary directions in policy, theory and practice in early childhood. *FORUM*, 49(1 & 2).

Wood, E. (2011) Listening to young children. Multiple voices, meanings and understandings. In Paige-Smith, A. and Craft, A. (eds) *Developing Reflective Practice in the Early Years*. Maidenhead: Open University Press, pp. 100–113.

Wood, E. (2013) *Play, Learning and the Early Childhood Curriculum*. 3rd edn. London: Sage.

Chapter 4

Levels of outdoor involvement

*Sally McMeeking, Moira Moran
and Danusia Taylor*

This chapter arose out of a Small Scale Research Project, funded by Nottingham Trent University, seeking to evaluate the possible impact of outdoor experiences on children's level of involvement in such learning activities. The chapter takes the form of a discussion between individuals, two practitioners and an academic, who are committed to offering children the opportunity to explore the affordances of the natural environment, and who are inspired by their observations of children's involvement in that environment.

The settings involved offer their children regular 'forest school' sessions. Although the delivery of the forest school experiences differs, and sessions may not adhere to all forest school principles (Knight, 2009), there are some common aspects of ethos that guide the practices and approaches.

Danusia is an early years professional (EYP) who owns and runs a rural preschool for children from babies to school age. The building is set at the edge of open countryside and the hedgerows sing with birds. Extensive grounds offer children a wide range of possibilities to play, explore and learn, including vegetable plots, a mud kitchen and loose parts for den building. Additionally, they visit a local well-managed Education Centre, which is run by a local charitable trust and whose aim is to provide outdoor learning for the local schools and early years settings. They have a fully trained forest school leader with them throughout the session and Danusia has attended some forest school training herself.

Sally is an EYP leading learning and development in a suburban city day nursery, which also provides for children from babies to school age. The nursery is set in spacious walled grounds containing mature trees and shrubbery, which create an attractive outdoor space for city children, hidden from the nearby main road. Children help to care for vegetables, which are used by the nursery cook or eaten raw for snack. There is a large sand pit and mud kitchen as well as an area of tarmac for bikes and other large wheeled toys; additionally Sally takes a small group of children by public transport one morning a week to the local park for a series of regular sessions. The sessions range throughout the park's varied areas and affordances according to the children's current dominant play and exploratory interest, with a small patch of woodland visited regularly on most sessions.

Moira has a background firmly rooted in the early years through teaching experience in nursery classes and a school, and more recently through the training of early years teachers and professionals, and in lecturing Childhood Studies students. Following training to Level 3 Certificate in Forest School Programme Leadership,

Moira has been able to introduce a module to the course that enables students to gain accredited forest school training as an addition to their degree through the affordances of the campus woodland.

M. Both settings, in different ways, have evidenced a commitment to supporting and extending the children's play, learning and development through engagement with a different and additional outdoor environment. Past conversations indicate that this has arisen from the practitioners' personal inclination towards the outdoors, from their personal experiences as mothers of active and exuberant sons (experiences shared by the academic) who loved *and needed* to be playing and learning outdoors and from their many years of observation of children's wellbeing and development in their settings.

This commitment to outdoor experiences for children would appear to reflect some contemporary concerns and messages expressed by a variety of national bodies advocating for children. The Council for Learning Outside the Classroom (LOtC, 2015) believes that 'every young person (0–19yrs) should experience the world beyond the classroom as an essential part of learning and personal development, whatever their age, ability or circumstances'.

Learning through Landscapes works with schools to support them in offering outdoor spaces for children's learning, and increasingly, protecting those spaces as the increasing number of children of school age in the United Kingdom puts those spaces under threat from buildings expansion. Play England, through the Playday campaign and the increasingly evident Street Play Project, amongst other ventures, 'campaigns for all children and young people to have freedom and space to play throughout childhood' (Play England, nd). The National Trust has built on its Natural Childhood report (Moss, 2012) promoting support for The Wild Network. The network advocates outdoor time for children to allow them to reconnect with nature, citing researched evidence of 'more than two thirds of primary school children ... suffering from back and neck pain', 'increasingly sedentary lifestyles that children are leading ... increasing their resting heart rates', and 'the prospect of a return of rickets as children have a lack of vitamin D, the best source of which is sunshine' (National Trust, 2013).

Learning outside the classroom

What are the special characteristics of this type of learning outside the 'classroom'?

D. The preschool owns a minibus, which we use to transport the children the 5 miles to the woodland setting. It is 'OUR' minibus, with our logo, our car seats and our special traditions, built up over the five years we have been going to forest school.

The children carry their own wellie baskets to the minibus, hand them to the adult (who loads them into the bus) and then go to the door on the side of the bus. They climb in, using the step and big yellow handle, choose their seats and strap themselves in, if they can. We then count down to the door closing – 1, 2, 3, scream! There are squeals of laughter as the door slams shut. This is part of the ritual and tradition; it is part of the 'culture 'of the setting, which one group of children passes down to the next.

Encounter: The journey

The journey starts with one of the children suggesting a song – as so often 'The wheels on the bus' is chosen. We sing about big tractor wheels, fast motorbike wheels, tiny scooter wheels and even the landing wheels on an aeroplane. We talk about how a helicopter hasn't got any wheels and that a lorry can have up to 12 wheels, some used as emergency wheels if one bursts. We discuss vehicles with two wheels and those with four, as well as steering wheels and brakes. This lasts until we arrive at the Centre, a full 15 minutes.

This sing-song is as large a part of the forest school trip as the woodland itself, sparking conversations that may not have been had indoors.

S. I was keen to try to follow the ethos of forest schools, with outdoor learning in green spaces a particular interest. As a city nursery we do not have easy access to a wood or many 'green' spaces; however, I discovered that a local park had the usual children's playground with swings and slides but it also had a small wooded area. It was also accessible from my setting by bus and that is where our adventure begins! We take a group of eight children with two adults. We catch a bus and talk about the numbers on the buses and why some dogs are allowed on. This leads to questions such as how the bus driver knows when to stop. We cross a busy road with much to talk about – the red man 'standing' and the green man 'walking' (and 'beeping') and walk the remainder of the way to the park. We pass a church, library and police station, all of which are good talking points, as are the shops, hairdressers and pubs! We notice and comment on graffiti and litter. Our journey is an adventure in itself.

Encounter: The wrong bus!

Peter found change very difficult to deal with. He had some communication difficulties and a limited vocabulary. I spoke to his mother regarding our trips to the park and how best to support him as he was a child who enjoyed being outdoors and his inclusion in the group was important to us. I showed Peter photos of the park and explained where we were going; however, I was not prepared for his reaction to the bus. He cried 'Wrong bus! Wrong bus! Not 25' throughout the whole of his first trip. He was very distressed and could not be consoled. I spoke to his mother and established that he caught the number 25 bus home each day. He was clearly able to recognise these familiar numbers. I showed Peter photos of our bus with the number 58 on and used simple explanations such as 'We are going to the park today. We need the 58 bus to take us to the park. Mummy will take you home on the 25 later'. Over his time with us Peter became our 'bus spotter' and was able to shout and laugh 'not 25 … that goes my home! Here 58 … go park!'

M. Here Peter is giving signals of Laever's aspect of involvement:

Verbal utterances

Children sometimes explicitly indicate that they are/were involved by their spontaneous comments … They can also indicate more implicitly that the activity appeals to them by giving enthusiastic descriptions of what they are/have been doing: they cannot refrain from putting into words what they are experiencing, discovering, …

(Laevers, 1994)

Rogers' (1983: 20) construct of experiential learning as cited previously by Woods would concur. He writes of it having

> *a quality of personal involvement* – the whole person in both feeling and cognitive aspects being *in* the learning event. It is *self-initiated*. Even when the impetus or stimulus comes from the outside, the sense of discovery, of reaching out, of grasping and comprehending, comes from within. *It is pervasive.* It makes a difference in the behaviour, the attitudes, perhaps even the personality of the learner.

Discovering and comprehending the possibility of a different 'right bus' involved Peter in personal learning that transformed his distress into spontaneous enthusiasm and a new role as expert within the community of the group.

These encounters evidence that the children's learning and engagement begins the minute they step out over the setting threshold to begin their adventurous journeys. It is a learning that appears grounded in culture and community, of the setting and of the community in which the setting sits. For the group on the mini-bus and for Peter, the individual, Laevers' (2006: 2) concept of involvement applies.

> The crucial point is that the satisfaction that goes along with involvement stems from one source, the exploratory drive, the need to get a better grip on reality, the intrinsic interest in how things and people are, the urge to experience and figure out.

Dahlberg *et al.* (2007: 23) further propose that 'the world and our knowledge of it are seen as *socially constructed* and all of us, as human beings, are active participants in this process … engaged in relationships with others in meaning making rather than truth finding'.

The experiences with the children on the journey to and from the site have been valued by practitioners who understand that 'When implementing experiential education, one starts where one stands' (Laevers, 2000: 28). The planned environment for play and learning is the woodland Education Centre or the local park respectively, but the community of travellers on the minibus, or the local community travelled through on the public bus also offer rich opportunities for real involvement, which cannot be ignored and should be valued, displaying as they do, signals of:

Energy

In motor activities physical energy is involved. ... In other activities a physical component may still catch the eye: (loud talking, shouting), the actions being carried out in a relatively short time ... Mental energy can become apparent in the zeal displayed in action or, more abstractly, in the (mental) effort showing on faces.

(Laevers, 1994)

Belonging and identity

> M. *Since these experiences are based in local community, and in the community of learners in the setting, how do they support those children who do not have a strong sense of belonging and identity in those groups, for whatever reason?*

S. All our children develop positive dispositions through our sessions in the park. I have never yet encountered a child who did not. For some it can be a very personal development, and can take some time.

Encounter: Aniya

Indoors Aniya is a confident and articulate only child. She especially enjoys role play, stories and writing. However, Aniya is reluctant to play outdoors and when she does she will choose similar activities to those she would choose indoors, reading, writing and role play. She was a late walker and walks up steps two feet to a step. She avoids all boisterous games and lacks the confidence to run, climb and balance. Her key person expressed some concerns regarding her gross motor skills.

Aniya always enjoyed the bus trip and going out of the setting; however, she would hold the practitioners hand for the duration of our visit to the park despite encouragement to do otherwise. Mum reports that they seldom have time for visits to the park.

Our 'eureka' moment was when her key person called a small bridge we passed on one occasion 'The Billy Goat Gruff Bridge'. Back at the setting Aniya recorded this as her favourite part of the park and told her mother about it. So we started having our snack at the bridge. We now always visit the bridge with Aniya and often act out the story of the Billy Goats or the Bear hunt there. Aniya loves these activities and is able to climb, run and balance with enthusiasm. On our last visit she even led the group saying; 'Follow me everyone, I'm the leader' in her rush to reach the bridge.

It has taken a year, and lots of encouragement but we now see a confident and exuberant Aniya.

For others it is a more social development, and can happen more quickly.

Encounter: Team work

Tayeeb and Fergus were in the youngest group of eight children to visit the park. Both children had a limited vocabulary and for Tayeeb, English was an additional language. These two boys only attended one session at preschool together and do not interact with each other within the setting. In fact observations showed that Fergus rarely initiated interactions with others. During our initial visits this very young group required much reassurance and support from the adults present. Further visits allowed the children to become more familiar with and therefore more confident within the environment. On one occasion just as we arrived inside the gate Fergus found a small log that he wanted to move. He was unable to move it himself and therefore enlisted the help of Tayeeb. The two boys negotiated and co-operated with each other taking turns to carry the log individually and when it became too heavy carrying it between them all around the park for the full duration of our visit. We heard the vocabulary 'you turn', 'me turn' and 'teamwork!' These two little boys continued to build on their friendship and widen their vocabulary with each trip to the park. Importantly this friendship was built upon when returning to the setting.

M. The image of Aniya chanting 'What a beautiful day! We're not scared.' (Rosen, 1993) as she leads her peers in play embodies the extent of her personal development through her engagement with the environment. It reflects Laevers' signal of:

Satisfaction

Activities possessing the quality of involvement often induce a feeling of 'satisfaction'. The source of this feeling may vary, but it must always imply 'exploration', 'getting a grip on reality', 'responding to certain stimuli'.

(Laevers, 1994)

The skill of the practitioner lay in the perceptive observation of the 'eureka moment', recognising how the actual physical bridge could act as a personal bridge in Aniya's development of belonging.

For Tayeeb and Fergus the development is different and equally significant. They take turns and work together. Their joint venture brings social collaboration to the task, and as a consequence, mastery. Stewart (2014) identifies collaboration as a common feature in a mastery-based goal and an important learning strategy that continues to have value throughout life.

Rogoff (1990: 199) as cited by Woods in Chapter 2 similarly states the enhanced potential of shared endeavour as they problem solve carrying the heavy log:

The mutual involvement of people working on similar issues is part of the social context of creativity. Dialogue, collaboration, and building from previous approaches often provide the catalyst for putting two ideas together that would not have occurred without the need for the individual thinker to carry out, explain, or improve on an approach.

Laevers (1994) also identifies the engagement signal of:

Reaction time

Young children are alert and easily respond to interesting stimuli …They also react to new stimuli occurring in the course of action, provided those are relevant.

The boys were seen actively displaying this signal. Aniya, Tayeeb and Fergus's engagement in activity during the park sessions enabled them to find their participatory role in the community of the setting. For the practitioner the reward was to see their identity as included and belonging carried back to the setting as well as to the park on the next visit.

Reflection and evaluation

M. *How have these reflections on outdoor experiences influenced subsequent practice?*

D. On one of our first trips to the forest school site, now many years ago, the children taught me a very important lesson. We were walking along the field edge to get to the woodland site. The children were intrigued by the long grass waving in the wind, running through it backwards and forwards and spotted an insect on the bramble bush. 'Does it hurt the beetle's feet on the prickles?' asked one child. I was keen to get to the woodland and start our 'session', so kept chivvying them along: 'Come on children, we need to get to base camp.'; 'We have to hurry or we won't have time in the wood.' The long grass and beetles were abandoned; however, when we returned to the setting and were reflecting on the session, it became obvious to me that we needed to give the children time to explore and investigate what interested them, for as long as they needed, and not follow the adult agenda or plan. The children were finding out about and investigating what they needed to discover, not what I thought they did. So now, we take our time and if we don't even get to the wood, so be it.

Encounter: Time to …

One of the children had stumbled whilst walking into the wood at the beginning of the session. What made you trip? 'It's a hole', said one of the children. 'It wasn't there last week', another said. A group of children then went on to discuss, in some depth and for some time, what might have made the hole and why. They agreed that it would be an animal of some type; 'too small for a badger, too big for a mouse' one girl suggested. Three of the children who were originally involved in the discussion moved onto something else, leaving four children to continue the discussion about the hole. 'I think it might be a rabbit', one suggested. 'Shall we dig and see if we can find it?' another asked. They went off to find some spades to dig out the rabbit. Two of the group dug for a little while then moved away – the remaining two children spent the whole session engrossed in digging. They were joined by other children occasionally, who stayed for a while then moved off, leaving the two girls to continue their search for the rabbit. They discovered roots, beetles, two spiders and a centipede – but no worms. They discovered that mud feels different when it has dried onto your hands and that rabbits can dig better than children. They learnt how to negotiate and listen to others' points of view – and all of this without ANY adult intervention.

M. It is possible to picture these two little children crouching close, intent on digging for the rabbit and discovering a myriad of other things instead. Laevers (1994) describes:

Concentration

The child is narrowing his/her attention to the limited circle of his/her activity. Only intense stimuli can reach and maybe distract him/her.
  and

Posture

The overall posture can reveal high concentration or boredom. Even when children are seen from the back only, one might assess the level of (non) involvement.

These children were respected as competent learners scientifically proposing their hypothesis for the hole based on prior knowledge of animals that make their homes underground, and allowed time to research and test that hypothesis. The children's project was enabled and given validity by a practitioner who realised through reflection that what is interesting to children will be the most engaging experience they can be offered, even though it may not always be what an adult would have planned or anticipated.

D. I have also come to believe that children are the best assessors of their own abilities. They 'know' when something is too easy or too difficult, they 'know' when they are ready to make an attempt at something that is challenging but just within their ever-increasing capabilities. I am continuously astounded at the ability of children of any age, from the very youngest of babies, to push themselves to meet and conquer these tough challenges – from learning to crawl and walk, to climbing a tree or riding a bike, to tying shoelaces or creating the most intricate of paintings. Children are driven to meet these challenges – it is Laevers' 'exploratory drive' in action. It is the task of the practitioner to recognise children's efforts and facilitate when, and if, they can.

Risk and challenge

Closely linked to this is children's ability to assess their own risk. Many times I have watched children approach the log rounds we have in our outdoor area and watch the older children step from log to log. If an adult approaches and asks if they would like to climb on, they shake their heads and wander away, still unsure of their ability to stay safe and unharmed. Too risky! But in time their confidence grows, they are more sure-footed and invariably they return to conquer the log rounds! We also have a 'hill' in our outdoor area with a tunnel running through it and this is another area where children's ability to assess their own risk is clearly evident. They appear to have an innate sense of where the edge is and its inherent danger. Most of the children stick to the middle; only those who have known the hill for some time venture near the edge, often flat on their stomachs, to look over the edge down to the tunnel below.

As a result of my thinking about risk and challenge I would never 'push' a child into doing something they did not want to do – they just might not be ready for the challenge – but I would always try to be there when they decided to make their first attempt.

Encounter: Risk and challenge

The children had headed towards the 'climbing trees', shouting about going on to 'the rocket' and into space. The 'climbing trees' are four parts of the same tree, which fell during some very windy weather and has been cut into four separate trunks. The biggest includes the up-rooted stump and is approximately 5 feet high, with the others each decreasing in size, with the smallest approx. 2 feet high – all are about 2 yards in length. They have been manoeuvred into position about a metre apart from each other and so resemble a series of show-jumping fences, increasing in difficulty. Most of the children already knew which they could climb with ease or with adult support. The older, larger children went straight for the 'cock-pit' of the rocket, sitting astride the tree with ease.

One little girl had never tried the climbing trees before and wasn't sure how to even start, looking very unsure. 'Would you like to try?' I asked. She nodded tentatively, looking a little afraid. With a suggestion to hold on and push herself up with her feet, she managed to climb onto the smallest trunk. She practised this, first with the adult and then without, for 10 minutes, by which time she had mastered it and gained confidence in her abilities. 'That one' she pointed to the next trunk and she did the same again – help from the adult, then on her own, then confident enough to move to a bigger challenge – until, at last, she was able to join in the voyage to space. This concerted effort took her about 45 minutes – she was so proud of herself it was the first thing mum heard about when she came to collect her.

M. Learning can be a risky business in itself, both for the child and for the observant practitioner, but risk-taking is recognised as an essential life skill for those innovators who will solve problems at local, national and global level. Rolfe (2010: 3) states:

'The experience of failure, as a result of risk taking in a safe environment, can help to build resilience to setbacks and help young people to manage risk better in the future.' Connor (2013) proposes that for these youngest children it is not through negative experiences that resilience is built, but rather through the reassuring presence of an 'emotionally aware caregiver' (Sunderland, 2006 in Connor, 2013: 118), nearby if needed, providing the safe environment in which these significant adventures can take place. The 'respectful educator' (Page *et al.*, 2013: 5) will value and affirm the efforts and achievements that have so much importance to the child, and crucially will allow the child time to display Laever's (1994) signals of:

Persistence

When concentrating, the child directs his full attention and energy towards one point. The moment this persistence refers and to the lengths of this concentration. Children who are involved do not easily let go of the action. They want the sensation of satisfaction, experienced with intense activity, to last and they are quite willing to do the necessary efforts. They are not easily distracted by minor activities. Activities possessing the quality of involvement tend to last (subject to age and levels of development).

Contemporary concerns

M. There are some challenges to the contemporary concerns and messages of what could be called the 'outdoor movement' discussed at the beginning of this chapter. Early years provision has undergone many changes recently, influenced by national policy changes implemented locally. The move towards an outcomes-based approach can be perhaps exemplified by the changes to statutory assessment for the Early Years Foundation Stage (DfE, 2014). The statutory requirement for completion of the EYFS Profile, assessed through practitioners' observed understanding of the holistic development of the unique child, will become voluntary after 2015. Replacing it is a reception baseline assessment:

> From the 2016 reception cohort onwards, the reception baseline assessment will be the only measure we use as the starting point for measuring progress to the end of key stage 2. We will hold schools to account at the end of key stage 2 by the attainment of their pupils and the progress they have made.
>
> (DfE, 2015)

Of the six DfE approved reception baselines only one takes a holistic approach, is observation-based, and makes reference to Characteristics of Learning (DfE, 2014) and to Laevers' dimensions of Wellbeing and Involvement (2006). All others involve models of testing, with predetermined questioning delivered through a 1:1 interview situation providing information that can readily be converted to a score for the child, allowing the measure of attainment and progress required by the Department for Education.

This move towards assessment against predetermined outcomes and standardised questions may impact on settings and practitioners with a potentially increasing pressure to teach to the test, as 'Our nets determine what we catch' (Eisner, 1985, in Blenkin and Kelly, 1992: 7). A move towards more adult-led activity, and away from child-led activity or child-initiated play may result, even in the earliest of early years settings. As previous chapters have shown, the process of learning can be regarded as of paramount importance.

Laevers (2007: 61) defines high levels of involvement:

> activities reflect the level of functioning attained by this particular person ... Involved persons are highly motivated. But we have to stress that the source of this motivation is the exploratory need, eagerness to understand and learn, the drive to get to grips with reality (in the literal and figurative sense of the word). Involvement always implicates intrinsic motivation.

Vygotsky (1978: 102) wrote of children's play: 'In play a child always behaves beyond his average age, above his daily behaviour. In play it is as though he were a head taller than himself' (Vygotsky, 1978: 102). This is echoed in Edwards *et al.*' (2010: 136) claim that: 'Process over product supports children's learning and knowledge acquisition. Process over product has been emphasised as an important component of learning, suggesting that the act of participation in play is more important than what the play itself generates.'

Forest school

The Forest School Association (FSA) expands Principle for Good Practice 6: 'Forest School uses a range of learner-centred processes to create a community for development and learning' by elucidating the criteria:

> A learner-centred pedagogical approach is employed by Forest School that is responsive to the needs and interests of learners.
>
> Play and choice are an integral part of the Forest School learning process, and play is recognised as vital to learning and development at Forest School.
>
> (FSA, nd)

Each of these sources would indicate the value of the child-led approach of an outdoor forest school model of experience for children.

> *How can the value of the child-led approach of an outdoor forest school model of experience for children be evidenced in and justified by practice?*

S. When first considering using a 'Forest School Approach' my idea was to take the children to a local wood and follow as closely as I could the ideas from my research regarding forest schools (with limitations as I am not a trained forest school leader and the wood we access is a public park!). My original research showed free and unstructured time in a wood; however, I realised that in the United Kingdom we often need a learning aim or outcome to our activities, and indeed I was questioned by both my manager and the setting owner as to the aim of my trips. They needed to see something tangible, preferably with something 'produced' at the end to show our parents!

To begin with I planned our park sessions, sometimes to the extent of printing off sheets of paper and taking clipboards to encourage the children to notice the environment, looking for signs of spring for example or different coloured leaves in autumn. The children enjoyed using the clipboards and pens initially but then became involved in their own activities. Within a short space of time the clipboards were handed over to the adults who either packed them away or attempted to re-engage the children. I discovered that children notice the environment without needing a clipboard and sheet of paper to tick. They need time to discover for themselves the wonders of our changing seasons, and sympathetic and sensitive adults to share in that wonder. In the summer we walk through a meadow with grass and wild flowers as tall as the children, we collect daises to make daisy chains. In the spring 'sticky' buds emerge on the 'climbing' branches that were previously bare. In winter frost covered cobwebs form on the fences of our shelter. Most enjoyable of all is the autumn when children gather so many conkers they can barely carry them all. We have a favourite tree – a horse chestnut or 'conker tree'. Throughout the seasons this tree provides us with all the loose parts we need for our exciting play; sticks for dens and camp fires, conkers, sticky buds, flowers and 'hand' leaves in a variety of vibrant colours.

Encounter: An open mind

Feeling pressure from colleagues and parents asking 'What did you do at the park today?' I felt the need to justify our trips by having a planned activity. These activities were adult-led and structured; for example, we would collect leaves and make crowns or take rubbings from trees. The children would take part in these activities but (I noticed) there was a fairly low level of involvement as they were easily distracted by their environment and would wander away to explore the area or become involved in other games. As the children became more familiar with their environment and I became more confident at recognising their learning, they began to lead the sessions and planned activities were abandoned. On one occasion on the way to 'our' wood we crossed an area of park where a large tree had been felled and was lying on its side, with several smaller logs around it. The children and I discussed why it was there and how it had got there. We stayed at this area for the whole of the session with children climbing and balancing on the large tree. One child decided the felled tree could be a train for us all to ride on. Two boys found smaller sticks and beat a large log like a drum, singing 'all aboard, all aboard'. One of the girls found some leaves and said 'You need tickets'. We now visit with an open mind instead of a planned activity.

M. The encounter in an environment of open-ended possibilities, where the children are allowed the time, space and control to make the tree trunk their own, offers us an example of Laevers' (1994) signal of:

Complexity and creativity

Children are at their best in activities accompanied by involvement. These activities are matching their competence. They fully apply to their cognitive and other capabilities. As a result, their behaviour is more than a routine behaviour. More often than not complexity involves creativity: the child adds an individual touch to the activity, he/she brings in his/her elements, produces something new, shows something not entirely predictable, something personal.

We can see the match to the children's 'cognitive and other capabilities'. There is social development, communication, language, physical development, creativity and understanding of the world in evidence. Children are displaying all of the Characteristics of Effective Learning and are engaging in sustained shared thinking with the adult and each other.

Trusting children

Additionally, this narrative of personal professional development and the encounter clearly evidence children's ability to lead their own learning through purposeful play experiences, play experiences that are purposeful to them rather than to an adult's decision about what is or is not purposeful. This handing-over of the role of decision maker to the children would seem to demand on the adult's part both a genuine trust in the children to be competent and capable to take on the role, and an authentic respect for children as active leaders of their learning.

S. Having taken groups of children to visit the wood in our local park over many years I do now rely on the children to make their own choices as to what we do when we arrive. These sessions are completely child-led without an 'outcome' in the minds of the adults present. We simply 'go with the flow'. On returning from the wood the children are invited to record their favourite activity in our electronic book using words, pictures and photos. This book is left out for everyone to look at and the children often discuss the various pages, activities and voices recorded. This can be used to make plans for the next visit; however, things often change upon our arrival at the wood as nature can give us some wonderful surprises!

Encounter: Children's choice

On one occasion the children were keen to visit an area they had discovered the previous week. However, it had been raining heavily and the children had such fun splashing in the massive puddles on the way that all other thoughts disappeared. Another time we visited when a meadow seemed to have sprung up overnight with grass and wild flowers as tall as the children. We played in the meadow for the whole session.

M. Again these encounters provide wonderful examples of children's deep involvement in activities that sustain their interest through being allowed choice as they 'get to grips with reality' (Laevers, 2007: 61). In both of these encounters sustained involvement and persistence can be seen as the natural environment afforded new provocations for exploration and learning. Occurrences that may seem commonplace or unremarkable to an adult – puddles after rain, meadow flowers growing in spring – are phenomena of real possibility for the children. The puddles are an example of the outdoor world as 'a dynamic place, where change, chance, serendipity, spontaneity, surprise and excitement are constantly available, especially with adults who are ready to respond to opportunity' (White, 2013: 51).

The opportunity to hide and lose oneself in a jungle of meadow flowers and grasses that seemed not to exist previously offers a sensory experience that can be explored and experienced in a multitude of different and individual ways, each of them rewarding and enriching. For some it may be the opportunity for active embodied learning as they experience physical movement through the environment of plants on a new scale, for others it may be a more detailed micro-exploration of the marvels and wonders of the natural phenomenon, for others again it may be a transformation into a fantasy world of imaginative play as the long wavy grass of Rosen's (1993) Bear Hunt comes to life before their eyes.

Moss and Petrie (2002: 5) reflect on an earlier work that proposed a discourse

> which foregrounded the child as a citizen, a member of a social group with rights, … as 'rich in potential, strong, powerful and competent'… with services conceptualised … [as a means] for enriching childhood, promoting children's culture and enabling children to participate in an essential world of relationships and activities…. a means for fostering the visibility, inclusion and active participation of all children in society.

It could be construed that the outdoor approaches of both of these settings exhibit the characteristics articulated by Moss, and in doing so, enable the active involvement of the children in meaningful and holistically enriching experiences supported by respectful educators.

Provocations

- Einstein wrote 'look deep into nature and then you will understand everything better'. To what extent do we offer opportunities for our children to explore *their* fascinations with the natural environment?
- Consider whether there is sufficient time for children to wallow in the outdoor affordances, or does our adult agenda direct experiences?
- In the adult team, who splashes in puddles, and who worries about muddy boots and wet legs?
- If there was one thing that could be done tomorrow that would enable children's engagement with the outdoor environment, what would it be?

References

Blenkin, G. and Kelly, A. (eds) (1992) *Assessment in Early Childhood Education.* London: Paul Chapman.

Connor, A. (2013) *Understanding Transitions in the Early Years. Supporting Change through Attachment and Resilience.* London: Routledge.

Dahlberg, G., Moss, P. and Pence, A. (2007) *Beyond Quality in Early Childhood Education Care and Education.* London: Routledge.

DfE (Department for Education) (2014) *Statutory Framework for the Early Years Foundation Stage.* Cheshire: Department for Education.

DfE (Department for Education) (2015) 2010 to 2015 Government policy: School and college funding and accountability. Appendix 2: Reception baseline assessment. Available at: https://www.gov.uk/government/policies/making-schools-and-colleges-more-accountable-and-funding-them-fairly/supporting-pages/reception-baseline-assessment (accessed 19 April, 2015).

Edwards, S., Cutter-Mackenzie, A. N. and Hunt, E. (2010) Framing play for learning. Professional reflections on the role of open-ended play in early childhood education. In Brooker, L. and Edwards, S. (eds) *Engaging Play.* Maidenhead: Open University Press, Chapter 10.

FSA (Forest School Association) (nd) Full principles and criteria for good practice. Available at: http://www.forestschoolassociation.org/full-principles-and-criteria-for-good-practice/ (accessed 19 February, 2015).

Knight, S. (2009) *Forest Schools and Outdoor Learning in the Early Years.* London: Sage.

Laevers, F. (ed.) (1994) *The Leuven Involvement Scale for Young Children, LIS-YC.* Manual and videotape. Leuven, Belgium: Centre for Experiential Education.

Laevers, F. (2000) Forward to basics! Deep-level learning and the experiential approach. *Early Years,* 20(2): 20–29.

Laevers, F. (2006) Making care and education more effective through wellbeing and involvement. An introduction to Experiential Education. Available at: http://cego.inform.be/InformCMS/custom/downloads/Ond_D%26P_IntroductionExpEduc.pdf (accessed 19 April, 2015).

Laevers, F. (2007) Deep level learning. An exemplary application on the area of physical knowledge. *European Early Childhood Education Research Journal,* 1(1): 53–68.

LOtC (Learning Outside the Classroom) (2015) Learning outside the classroom changes lives ... Available at: http://www.lotc.org.uk/ (accessed 12 March, 2015).

Moss, P. (2012) Natural childhood. Available at: https://www.nationaltrust.org.uk/document-1355766991839/ (accessed 7 January, 2014).

Moss, P. and Petrie, P. (2002) *From Children's Services to Children's Spaces. Public Policy, Children and Childhood.* London: RoutledgeFalmer.

National Trust (2013) Celebrities support The Wild Network campaign. Available at: http://www.nationaltrust.org.uk/article-1355814114602/ (accessed 7 January, 2014).

Page, J., Clare, A. and Nutbrown, C. (2013) *Working with Babies and Children.* 2nd edn. London: Sage.

Play England (nd) Campaigns. Available at: http://www.playengland.org.uk/our-work/campaigns.aspx (accessed 12 March, 2015).

Rogers, C. (1983) *Freedom to Learn for the 80's.* 2nd edn. Columbus, OH: Charles E. Merrill.

Rogoff, B. (1990) *Apprenticeship in Thinking. Cognitive Development in Social Context.* New York: Oxford University Press.

Rolfe, H. (2010) *Learning to Take Risks, Learning to Succeed.* London: NESTA.

Rosen, M. (1993) *We're Going on a Bear Hunt.* London: Walker Books.

Stewart, N. (2014) Active learning. In Moylett, H. (ed.) *Characteristics of Effective Early Learning. Helping Young Children Become Learners for Life.* Maidenhead: Open University Press, pp. 54–71.

Vygotsky, L. S. (1978) *Mind in Society.* Cambridge, MA: Harvard University Press.

White, J. (2013) Capturing the difference. The special nature of the outdoors. In White, J. (ed.) *Outdoor Provision in the Early Years.* London: Sage, pp. 45–57.

Chapter 5

The role of practitioner engagement in supporting children's involvement

Vicky McEwan

The relationship between the child, the adult and the environment is key to both developing and sustaining children's involvement in their play. We know that children will naturally play anywhere and with anything as they have a natural exploratory drive to explore, discover, re-create and ask questions; as practitioners our role is to encourage this, to create optimum opportunities, to extend and to stimulate. Laevers and Moons (1997) acknowledge this key adult role in the Ten Action Points that they developed to raise involvement, as discussed earlier by Brown in Chapter 4. The Ten Action Points refer to considering the layout of the room, the relationships between children, the planned experiences, and also the adult's support by 'stimulating [children's] impulses and enriching interventions' (Laevers and Moons, 1997). Laevers *et al.* (1997) developed an Adult Style Observation System (known as the ASOS) to help us observe adults' 'style'; this provides us with a tool to look at the patterns in the way adults respond to children or intervene in a wide variety of situations. The ASOS is built around the three dimensions of stimulation, sensitivity and autonomy. This chapter will explore practitioner engagement, considering why it is such an essential element in children's involvement.

The Effective Provision of Pre-School Education (EPPE) project, found that where staff showed warmth and were responsive to children that children made better progress (Sylva *et al.*, 2004). In 2004 when the EPPE project published these findings very few settings routinely used peer observation, but now there are many tools and methods widely available for observing adults in a setting. This chapter will explore adult engagement using a range of encounters to unpick and capture the qualities that make an engaging interaction, asking questions such as how warm was the adult, how present and available were they, how did they stimulate the child's thinking, how much independence did they allow, and how did they respond to the child's communication? It will consider how to develop a system of peer observation and reflection that is meaningful to the setting as a whole and supportive to an individual staff member's development. When used effectively peer observation can become a sound foundation to build what Wenger (1998) would describe as a 'community of practice' in a setting.

Why does adult engagement matter?

In considering why adult engagement matters we will first look at the work of Rogers (1983). In Chapter 1, Woods discusses Rogers' 'fully functioning person' and how Laevers has drawn on these ideas in his work on the highly involved child; we can also see the work of Rogers reflected in Laevers' work on teacher style. Rogers identified what he called a set of 'attitudinal qualities which exist in the personal relationship between the facilitator and the learner' (Rogers, 1983: 106). Rogers cites three groups of attitudinal qualities:

1 realness or genuineness;
2 prizing, accepting and trust;
3 empathetic understanding.

We will discuss these qualities later in the chapter when we consider the work of Laevers *et al.* (1997) and Pascal and Bertram (2003). Here, let us consider the why rather than the what: why is it important to have these facilitative qualities in the adults that work with children?

Rogers (1983) cites a study by Aspy and Roebuck (1969) where teachers were trained in facilitative qualities to offer high levels of empathy, congruence and positive regard; they found that where teachers used these qualities the children gained in a range of ways, including being more creative, more spontaneous, displaying higher thinking levels, greater academic achievement and having an increased positive self-regard. They also found that the benefits were cumulative, so the longer the child experienced these qualities in their teaching the greater the gains.

Formosinho (2003) discusses the importance of interactions and cites a range of international studies that focus on the interactions of the early years teacher. In a study by Phillips *et al.* (1987), cited by Formosinho, they found that the amount of time children aged between three and six years old spent on verbal interaction with the teachers strongly related to their development in language, intellectual, and social competence, how sociable they were and the consideration they were able to show towards others. Formosinho also discusses a study by Holloway and Reicjardt-Erickson (1998) where it was found that a teacher who was respectful, responsive, engaging and democratic led to children who were able to resolve social problems. Formosinho (2003: 119) develops her ideas as she discusses a number of studies where teachers had a direct or punitive style and this led to children having poorer cognition and co-operative skills; she concludes that 'this selection of studies shows how important the teacher's style of interaction is. In fact, the influence of interaction style can be felt both in children … and in the [social] environment the teacher creates.'

In a more recent longitudinal study carried out in the United Kingdom by Sylva *et al.* (2004) looking at the effective provision of pre-school education (EPPE Project), they found a number of factors relevant to the discussions here; first that the quality of the pre-school directly impacts on the children's intellectual and social/behavioural development and that these benefits continue into primary education. A further study by Sylva *et al.* in 2008, found that these benefits lasted to the end of Key Stage 2 for attainment in Reading/English and Mathematics; the study also found that the children who attended medium to high quality pre-schools had improved social/behavioural outcomes at this age. Further research by Sylva *et al.* (Sammons *et al.*, 2014) provided some statistical evidence to show that there was still a continuing positive impact on children's social/behavioural outcomes at age 16, although they acknowledge that the effects here were small; however, Sylva *et al.* (2014) did find that the quality of pre-school predicted both total GCSE scores and English and Mathematics grades and they were also able to make links with the higher quality pre-school education and high levels of self-regulation.

In the first study Sylva and her team (2003) found that the quality of the adult–child verbal interactions where staff encouraged sustained shared thinking was a significant factor in the most effective early years practice; we can make links here with stimulation on the Laevers *et al.* (1997: np), adult engagement scale, that looks for adults 'confronting [children] with thought provoking questions and giving them information that can capture their mind' as an indicator of stimulating engagement. Sylva *et al.* (2003: 4) noted that 'the quality of the interactions between staff and children were particularly important; where staff showed warmth and were responsive to the individual needs of children, children showed better social behavioural outcomes'.

This clearly supports Rogers' early thinking on the attitudinal qualities needed to be a facilitative educator.

In conclusion we can see that there is a wealth of evidence that suggests the quality of the adults' engagement with children is of vital importance to their long-term holistic development.

Core elements of adult engagement with children

Encounter: Tea time ... more please!

In a busy day nursery the children in the toddler room are having their tea of toast and milk. The children sit around the table without plates, eating directly from the table surface. The adults stand chatting at the side, one child asks for more toast: 'More please', holding up his hand. An adult picks up the plate and takes it over to the table, she throws a slice of toast over the heads of the children sitting directly in front of her over to the child that requested more, he snatches it up and eats it, she returns to chat to other staff.

This encounter was observed by an early years adviser some years ago who was visiting the nursery. The children in the encounter were being cared for by adults, but the adults appeared to be indifferent to their needs. Many settings at that time were not providing quality experiences for the children (Ofsted, 1998). At the time of writing the latest Ofsted inspection reports for the period 1 April, 2014 – 30 June, 2014 found that out of 4,952 full inspections of childcare provision 18 per cent required improvement. These figures highlight that we unfortunately still have settings that do not provide the best for the children and whilst we must acknowledge that these inadequate inspections may be down to issues that may not directly impact on the experiences of the children it does raise concerns about the overall quality of the settings children are in today.

In the next section of this chapter we will consider the qualities or core elements we *should* look for in early years practitioners.

In looking at the elements of engagement we will explore the work of Pascal and Bertram, who have developed an Adult Engagement scale to be used within the Effective Early Learning (EEL) project (1997) and the Baby Effective Early Learning (BEEL) project (2005); for this they have drawn heavily upon the work of Laevers'

Experimental Education project and the Adult Style Observation Schedule (1997). Bertram (1996: 116) explains that the EEL framework is symbiotic and negotiated, because not only does the adult style of engagement impact on the child's involvement but the child's involvement affects the adult's engagement. Bertram debates and defines the meaning of the word 'engagement':

> Engagement may be defined as a set of personal qualities which describe the nature of the educative relationship between the adult and the child. These personal qualities will affect an adult's ability to motivate, extend, enhance and involve the children in the learning process.
>
> Bertram (1996: 116)

Pascal and Bertram (1997) describe three core elements, taken from the work of Laevers *et al.* (1997), when observing a teacher's style (although they refer to teachers the project is carried out widely in a range of settings, and they use the term for any adult working with the children). These elements are used to define the quality of the interactions with the children, with practitioners placed along an engagement scale from 'totally engaging' to 'totally non-engaging' qualities for each element. Sensitivity, stimulation and autonomy are the three core elements or qualities; below we look at each in turn.

> **Sensitivity:** This is the sensitivity of the adult to the feelings and emotional well-being of the child and includes elements of sincerity, empathy, responsiveness and affection.
>
> (Pascal and Bertram, 2003: 82)

Laevers *et al.* (1997: np) write:

> Sensitivity is evidenced in responses that witness empathic understanding of the basic needs of the child, such as, the need for security, for affection, for attention, for affirmation, for clarity and for emotional support.

Sensitivity is a key element of early years practice, there is no other profession in which we are expected to give love in such an open but professional way. The following encounters help us to explore sensitivity.

Encounter: Good morning Freya

Freya is arriving at her childminders with her parent. The childminder opens the door and immediately smiles, her face radiates warmth and a genuine welcome to the child and her parent; she opens the door widely to let them in and says, 'Good morning Freya, I'm so glad you're here, Bert-Bert (the rabbit) has been waiting for his breakfast and now you're here we can go and feed him together'. The child smiles and runs off

> to get the food pots. The childminder and the parent exchange information and then the parent kisses Freya goodbye. The childminder and Freya go off to feed the rabbit chatting about the activities they will do that day; they are holding hands.

This encounter is high in elements of sensitivity, demonstrated by the childminder's use of the child's name, facial expressions and body language, giving the child a sense that they are needed and important in the setting. The childminder was also acknowledging that separating from parents was a difficult thing for Freya and by giving her a task that she enjoyed distracted her from the separation, which in turn supported her emotional well-being at a time when it was often low. This empathy with the child's needs and concerns is a key indicator outlined by Pascal and Bertram (1997) of sensitive engagement.

Encounter: Help, help

Eden is developing her self-feeding skills. She has managed to feed herself a pot of yogurt but is unable to scrape the last few bits out of the pot; after several attempts, she gets up and takes her pot and spoon to her mother saying, 'Help, help', and handing her the spoon and pot. Her mother takes the pot and spoon and comments: 'Wow, did you do all that yourself, you are very clever at that, would you like some help with the last bit?' Eden nods and smiles. Mum takes her by the hand and sits next to her at the table; she puts her arms around Eden so they can hold the pot and spoon together, she puts the remaining yogurt on the spoon and hands it back to Eden to eat.

One of the indicators for sensitivity suggested by Pascal and Bertram (1997) is that they encourage the child to trust, and in this encounter the child clearly seeks out a trusted adult to help her with a task she is unable to do alone. The adult is sensitive with this trust and acknowledges her achievements so far and allows Eden to continue to develop her independence whilst sensitively supporting her. Her mother is demonstrating her ability to do what Bion (nd) would have referred to as 'containing' the child's emotional communications; she understands Eden's concerns and communicates them back to her and makes herself emotionally available to Eden, as together they overcome the problem. This encounter is also an example of what Rogoff (1990) terms as guided participation, to describe how children learn through being with an adult in a real-life social exchange. Guided participation is important as it is through this interpersonal interaction and exchange that children move from dependence to independence.

We see in both these encounters elements of physical contact, in holding hands and putting arms around a child. Physical contact is important to young children to demonstrate your affection towards them and it is of great concern that many schools and settings have a no physical contact rule, brought about from a prevalent culture of fear and litigation as a result of (too many) high profile cases. In order to be sensitive Pascal and Bertram (1997) suggest we look for adults that are warm and demonstrate affection towards children.

Let us turn now to the second element or dimension of teacher style, Stimulation.

> **Stimulation:** This is the way in which the adult intervenes in a learning process and the content of such intervention.
>
> (Pascal and Bertram, 2003: 82)

Laevers *et al.* (1997: np) write:

> Stimulating interventions are open impulses that engender a chain of actions in children and make the difference between low and high involvement. Such as: suggesting activities to children that wander around, offering materials that fit in an ongoing activity, inviting children to communicate, confronting them with thought provoking questions and giving them information that can capture their mind.

For the child to receive stimulation when we are using the adult engagement scale there must be a direct interaction with the child. We are looking for an exchange where the adult provides stimulation rather that the setting up of a stimulating environment for a whole group of children, for whilst this is important, it is looking here at something that will have an effect of supporting a child's involvement in a task, thus raising their individual involvement indicators, something we can measure and quantify. The following encounters help us explore stimulation.

Encounter: Brooklyn and the parachute

Brooklyn is new to the Music group, he sits in a circle with his mother initially but soon tires of this and begins to get up and wander around the room; he is not engaged in the singing and actions the other children and parents are doing lead by the teacher. His mother brings him back several times to the group but he repeatedly gets up and wanders. The teacher gets out a parachute and asks Brooklyn to come and hold the handle next to her; he does and soon he is actively involved in moving the parachute in a variety of ways, as the teacher encourages him, giving him praise and attention for his efforts, making suggestions about moving it to make a big, big balloon, which clearly interests him as he shouts 'up, up!'. His involvement has soared from roaming non-engagement, to enthusiastic engagement displaying high levels of involvement in the activity.

The teacher successfully engaged Brooklyn with a very simple act of suggesting he held the handle, by placing him next to her she was also being sensitive to his need for attention and support. The teacher realised he needed a more active activity and selected the point of introducing the parachute to involve him, recognising that this would be the activity that would hook him in; the suggestion that the parachute was a big balloon clearly stimulated his interest and he used his language to display his involvement.

In this next encounter we see the adult intervening with a question that stimulates the child to think.

Encounter: What would happen if ...

Amari has been playing in the large sandpit outside, she has found a pretty pebble and buries it and then digs it up; her key person notices this and asks her about her pretty stone. Amari calls it her treasure. The key person asks what would happen if Amari forgot where she had buried it. Amari thinks for a moment and then says, 'I'll put the stick on to save the place'. The key person replies: 'Oh like a pirate, marking an X on a treasure map, what a good idea'; they talk about treasure maps for a few moments. The key person leaves and then returns with some clipboards and pencils: 'Amari, I've got these for you if you wanted them.' Amari replies: 'I'll make a pirate map, then I'll always be able to find my treasure'. Amari picks up the materials and begins to make a map.

The adult's question here of 'What would happen if ...?' followed by the bringing of additional materials moved Amari's activity from one that although she was interested in was not challenging her mentally; with the adult's intervention she needed to think of a way to find her pebble again and also to help her remember where it was. By adding a clipboard and pencil, the activity allowed her to communicate her ideas and extend it further.

Stimulating intervention to raise a child's involvement in an activity does come with caution as sometimes our intervention is not welcome; we will all have experienced going over to an activity and engaging ourselves only to find that a few minutes later the children have all left the activity. The key to intervention that is stimulating is timing; we must watch and only intervene when we feel that our question, suggestion or involvement will extend, sustain or develop what is already happening.

We will now move to our third element/dimension of giving children autonomy.

Autonomy: This is the degree of freedom, which the adult gives the child to experiment, make judgements, and choose activities and express ideas. It also includes how the adult handles conflict, rules and behaviour issues.

(Pascal and Bertram, 2003: 82)

Laevers *et al.* (1997: np) write:

Giving autonomy is not only realised in the open form of organisation but has to be implemented as well at the level of interventions. It means: to respect children's sense for initiative by acknowledging their interests, giving them room for experimentation, letting them decide upon the way an activity is performed and when a product is finished, implicate them in the setting of rules and the solution of conflicts.

Autonomy includes giving children independence to learn and discover but this must be in an active rather than passive interaction. It is not sufficient to suggest that by giving children total freedom in the environment we are supporting autonomous learners, because learners need more than an environment, they need adults that encourage them to explore and experiment, to listen to the questions they ask and in turn ask their own questions, to encourage them to be reflective and assess their own work and to make decisions about their own learning. The engagements we will see when looking at autonomy will relate closely to the characteristics of effective learning (DfE, 2012): playing and exploring, active learning, and creating and thinking critically.

Encounter: Zip the robot

At three years old Darcey is an accomplished model maker; at home she has an extensive making corner with workshop style self-accessing materials including paint, glue, tape, boxes, various collage materials, etc. She chooses to spend her time at both the childminders and home engaged in making activities. Darcey has recently been interested in the book Harry and the Robots by Ian Whybrow and also an electronic robot head with simple computer games called Zip at her Nana's house. Darcey spies her Mum throwing out a large cardboard box and asks if she can have it; she takes it to her making corner where she begins to rummage in a tub of boxes; Mum sees her and asks if she needs anything. Mum's offer of help is accepted and Mum is sent to find a box smaller than this but bigger than this and not too square. Mum returns with a selection of boxes including a hexagonal flat tray box that had contained a clock. Darcey seizes the box declaring it perfect for Zip's head; she is making a robot called Zip. Mum sits close by watching and supports holding things still and cutting tape when instructed. Mum sometimes asks questions to support the secure fixing of things; for example, when the glue stick won't hold up a googly eye, Mum asks what else we have that is good at sticking things and gets out some sticky tack, string, and parcel tape; the sticky tack is selected. After some time the robot is declared finished. He looks great says Mum, what can he do? For a moment Darcey is quiet and appears to be serious and deep in thought; she then replies that she still needs to do that bit. Over the coming weeks and months additional pieces are added to Zip as he gains a variety of functions including buttons with numbers to make phone calls, letter stickers for writing messages and hands for holding things. Zip is large and difficult to house for such a long time but Darcey's Mum respects the ongoing building, and carefully puts him up high at the end of each making session. After several weeks pass where Darcey does not make any additions to Zip Mum asks how Zip is coming along and Darcey replies that he is finished but needs to be kept in the cellar for now. Occasionally, even nine months after he was first built, he is taken out and something added or taken away.

In this encounter we see Darcey's Mum supporting her building in a range of ways; she allows total freedom of resourcing but supports this decision-making by providing additional materials, she allows exploration and experimentation as additional functions are considered. She also allows Darcey to decide when Zip is finished and agrees to him being kept but not left out, thus allowing Darcey to make her own judgements and reflect on his progress. This all leads to a series of interactions where Darcey is actively supported to be autonomous.

Encounter: I had that!

In a reception class the children have been read the story of The Lighthouse Keeper's Lunch by Ronda and David Armitage, and have been tasked with designing and making a system to get the lunch to the lighthouse without the seagulls being able to eat the food. They are working in pairs supported by a classroom assistant. Josh and Madison have been using some fabric that they are tying on to their basket; another pair, Josie-Mae and Louis working close by pick up the fabric and begin to cut a strip off it. 'Oi! That's ours!' shouts Josh, snatching it back and sending the scissors flying. The classroom assistant, Miss Green, comes over and asks what the problem is; they all begin to talk at once and Josie-Mae cries. Miss Green takes Josie-Mae's hand and asks all four to stop talking and then she asks Josh to explain first. She tells them that they will each get a turn to talk. After listening to them all in turn she asks, 'So what should we do?' and waits. Louis says that perhaps he and Josie-Mae could find some different fabric from the box; Josie-Mae cries again she wanted the blue fabric. Madison suggests that they give them one strip of their fabric and then help them to find another piece of blue. This seems to be accepted by everyone and Miss Green praises them for great sharing and moves away as they all become involved in looking in the fabric box.

In this encounter, it would have been easy and much quicker for Miss Green to insist the fabric was shared out immediately and they return to their designs but she demonstrated giving autonomy as she gave each child time to explain the situation from their perspective and then without giving any judgements on the situation she asked the question: 'So, what should we do?' This encouraged the children to find a solution and negotiate, which they did whilst being sensitive to Josie-Mae. Miss Green also demonstrated sensitivity in holding Josie-Mae's hand to reassure and calm her. The quality of autonomy is very important in encouraging negotiation and conflict resolution, and by teaching the children to listen to each other and come up with a solution together, the adult was teaching them to work through the problem without needing an adult to solve the problem. In the future this may help them to solve conflict without the need of an adult, therefore teaching them to be autonomous.

As we have seen from these encounters the three dimensions are often used together and at times one style will be more appropriate than others depending on the situation. For example, in 'Brooklyn and the parachute' we see the adult using sensitivity and stimulation but it is not appropriate to have used autonomy; we could suggest that Brooklyn was given little opportunity to be autonomous or experiment with the parachute as the teacher very clearly suggested how to move the parachute. There was nothing wrong with him having limited autonomy at that point and we should not expect to see practitioners always scoring highly along scales for all elements. Laevers *et al.* (1997) suggest that in using the ASOS we will see how a teacher's intervention will vary depending on the nature of the activities as well as the children themselves, a symbiotic exchange (Bertram, 1996).

Peer observation in settings

In this section we will discuss how peer observation came to be used in settings and the benefits of introducing it to both the setting as a whole and the individual staff members. Many settings acknowledge the importance of the child, adult, environment triangulation by using a reflective practice approach that considers not just what, but how the children are learning, how the environment supports them in this learning and how the adults in the setting scaffold and encourage children in the process of learning. In the past many local authorities supported schools and settings to work towards quality assurance schemes as a kite mark of their effectiveness, to raise the quality of their practice and to evidence their commitment to providing these quality services to the children and families they served. Mooney (2007: 5) writes that:

> In England, following the launch of the National Childcare Strategy and an emphasis on improving the quality of ECEC [Early Childhood Education and Care], there was a greater interest among national professional organisations and local authorities in using quality assurance schemes as a means to raise standards.

As part of the Investors in Children endorsement, quality assurance schemes had to meet a set of criteria; peer observation was part of the criteria for a scheme to be endorsed.

> Supporting providers to undertake systematic observations of staff working with children is an essential element of assessing the quality of experiences for children. QA schemes should include materials that will help providers explore the quality of adult/child interactions in their setting, and encourage them to reflect and evaluate their own practice.
>
> (DfES, 2002: 8)

Many settings first introduced peer observation as part of a quality assurance scheme and this was then an element that became embedded in their practice because they found it to be a powerful tool for improving not only the practice of individuals but the provision as a whole.

Pascal and Bertram (2003) in evaluating the effectiveness of the EEL project found that adult engagement in all three elements – sensitivity, stimulation and autonomy – increased during the EEL process of evaluation and improvement. Settings that carried out the EEL project continued to use this as part of an ongoing cycle of refection and improvement. The training in peer observation was also valued by the settings and Pascal and Bertram (2003: 90) found that 'all [types of] settings respond to training and those settings with less qualified staff make the greatest progress'. The encounter below is one manager's reflections on the introduction of peer observations as part of the EEL and BEEL projects in her setting.

Encounter: Do we have to do it?

The deputy and I had been on the training for peer observation as part of the EEL and BEEL project we were doing. We discussed it with the staff at a meeting. They were all worried about it and one member of staff asked if she 'had' to do it. We listened to their concerns and tried to address them; we followed it up with training using the EEL and BEEL clips and having a go as a group, which they enjoyed doing because it was safe, it wasn't about them. We observed the adults alongside the children's observations we were doing for the project. At the end of the day we told them what we had done and gave them all their observations to read; they were all really pleased with their outcomes that showed they were using high levels of engagement. From then on they all became involved in carrying out the observations. After the project we discussed the process as a team and they all wanted to keep going with peer observations because they enjoyed them, they found they learnt from watching others and they liked supporting each other, and so we embedded it in our supervision and appraisal system.

A project focusing on 'Developing Quality through Leadership', funded by the National Strategies and published in 2007, documents the progress of six settings introducing peer observation. The settings all received training on both reflective practice and peer observation, which the senior staff had to cascade back to their teams. The settings were also encouraged to plan time for the observations to take place and sufficient staff:child ratios to ensure the running of the setting was not compromised. The impact of introducing the peer observation systems was very beneficial and all six settings continued to use it as part of their practice; they also documented that as a result of the observations the provision was developed, with the project acting as a 'catalyst for change'. There were clear developments and improvements for leaders, staff, children and parents; considering the impact on staff is particularly valuable, staff reported:

- feeling 'empowered' and 'inspired': everyone's contribution is valued;
- feeling a greater sense of belonging, more ownership of what is happening in their setting;
- better communication through improved teamwork;
- greater confidence, especially in planning and understanding next steps for children;
- improved observational skills;
- developing their own leadership skills because of greater delegation: 'natural leaders' have emerged;
- more interest shown by staff in training and professional development;
- more involvement in evaluating what they do;
- [improved] literacy skills.

(National Strategies, 2007)

There are some very powerful developments here for staff that would benefit not only the individual but all those in the setting. These feelings and developments by the staff members in both the above encounter and in the National Strategies project demonstrate an effective community of practice. Wenger (nd) defines a community of practice as 'a group of people who share a concern or a passion for something they do and learn how to do it better as they interact regularly'. Wenger (1998) discusses how people make the difference in an organisation; this is very true in an early years setting where the quality of the experience in the setting is dependent on the people, the practitioners, who work there. Wenger (1998: 253) explains that it is when we are learning in that community that we are able to make a difference, and to contribute to the development of our practice in settings:

> What we learn with the greatest investment is what enables participation in the communities with which we identify. We function best when the depth of our knowing is steeped in an identity of participation, that is, when we can contribute to shaping the communities that define us as knowers.

The development of staff as individuals and a community of practice, along with the knowledge we have on the long-term benefits to children's holistic development, provides us with a clear rationale for using a system of peer observation in our settings. In the next part of this chapter we will consider how to develop a system of peer observation in our settings.

Developing a system of peer observation in your setting

In this section we will consider the introduction of peer observations in five clear stages:

1   prior discussions and decision-making about the process and format to be used;
2   training for the whole team;
3   carrying out the observations;
4   feeding back after the observation to support individual development;
5   reflecting on the observations in terms of the setting as a whole and evaluating the process.

1 Prior discussions

- In developing a system of peer observation we need to first provide staff with a clear rationale: why are we doing this, why is it important to us and what do we hope to achieve from it? This is best done as a whole staff team to allow everyone to hear the messages together and ask questions.
- The next step is to consider a selection of formats and approaches that can be considered and evaluated for use in your setting. There are a wide selection of formats available but you need to consider what is right for your context; avoiding ones that are over complex will mean that you will be more likely to use them. The best formats are those that are developed by the staff teams themselves, so have a look and pick the bits you like from a number of systems and formats. Those with prompts or clear criteria for making judgements (such as the ASOS or EEL model) will support staff development and provide consistency and rigour in judgements that are made. It is also important to consider how long you will observe for: will it be for two minutes, three times in one session, or one longer five-minute observation in a session?

- Many settings also use a pre-observation sheet where observers and the observed can discuss and agree where they wish to be observed; for example, a member of staff may wish to be observed during a story time as they feel this is an area they struggle with, or an element of their practice they could develop.
- It is at this point staff may wish to buddy into pairs to carry out the process; however, a word of caution, as it may be more supportive to go with someone who you respect and whose practice you value rather than a best friend who may not feel able to be honest.
- You also need to make decisions here as a staff team about what will happen to the observations: will they be kept in staff files, or used as evidence for appraisals?

2 Training for the whole team

- Once you have a format you are happy with you need to train the staff in using the system.
- It is best to watch some clips of child–adult exchanges and have a practice as a group, with each member of staff completing the observation sheet individually then discussing and agreeing judgements.
- The judgements need to be consistent across the team and it may take more than one training session to ensure consistency and rigour in the judgements that are being made.
- After you have used some generic clips you may feel confident enough to video yourselves and use these to practice with as a whole team; this can be more meaningful because you are able to discuss with more insight into the children and the situation.
- Training on feedback should be given at this point and giving feedback should also be practiced with staff role playing, giving and receiving feedback. After role playing feedback discussions can be encouraged about how they felt giving and receiving the feedback; some staff may need additional support with this and it may be necessary for some paired observations and feedback sessions to be carried out with some staff to ensure quality, supportive and professional feedback is given.

3 Carrying out the observations

- Once all staff members are happy with the format and system to be used you should plan in time for the observations to take place. You should ensure it is recorded on planning sheets that staff are to be released to carry out observations; extra cover may be needed to ensure ratios and the running of the setting is not compromised.
- In observing you should be honest and record exactly what you see.
- You should also spend some time after the observation making sure that you have captured everything and considering your judgements using the chosen criteria.

4 Feeding back after the observation to support individual development

- Time should also be planned in to release both members of staff to discuss the observation; this should be as close to the observation as possible as it will still be fresh in their minds and also bear in mind that having to wait for feedback can cause unnecessary anxiety.

- The person observed should be asked how they felt the session went and given time to evaluate their own practice first.
- Observations need to be honest and open.
- When giving feedback the emphasis is on encouraging the positives, being explicit about points for development and prioritising these.
- Feedback should always be confidential and observation outcomes are not for general consumption.
- Feedback should be professional and supportive.
- Observations and feedback should help foster positive working relationships between colleagues; for example, you may suggest after watching a member of staff lead a story time session that they may want to watch another member of staff who is really good at storytelling and drama.
- Feedback should be followed up with professional development opportunities; so, for example, if the member of staff was found to be over directive during outdoor play they may be able to go and see other settings that you know have outdoor environments where children are encouraged to take risks.

5 Reflecting on the observations in terms of the setting as a whole and evaluating the process

- Once the observations have been carried out the management team should consider the whole picture and ask questions about what this tells you about your practice. For example, if sensitivity was high across the board but autonomy was low you may need to do some staff training on developing children's autonomy, or consider if you are you offering too many adult–directed activities. Perhaps you are too focused on end products, so that practitioners feel that they have to get children to produce an end product to take home or evidence in their books, leaving the children little opportunity for exploration and play.
- The management team should also ensure all training needs from individuals are supported to ensure that staff in your setting feel they have been supported in their development and that the process has been beneficial to them. Remember training doesn't have to mean going on a course; it can be observing someone in your setting, being given a paper to read or a clip to watch and then discussing it with a colleague, or it can be visiting another setting.
- The whole team should also sit down together and reflect on the process. It may also be helpful to give staff an evaluation sheet to fill in about how they found the process. Again the management team should reflect on these evaluations.
- Finally, decisions should be made about how you will continue with the peer observation system, considering all the factors from evaluations.

This chapter has provided a clear rationale for looking at adult engagement and carrying out peer observations. We have identified the long-term benefits to children's holistic development that having staff that are sensitive, stimulating and who provide autonomy for children can have. We have considered the impact on staff individually and collectively of being part of the process on peer observations and we have given clear guidelines on how to establish a working system in your setting. The provocations will provide you with opportunity to consider this chapter and can also be used with other staff to open up discussions on adult engagement and peer observations.

Provocations

- Who has been the colleague you have learnt most from? What was it you learnt from them? What qualities did they have? How have you used what you learnt?
- Consider when you saw a child really engaged in an activity with an adult, what was that adult doing? Consider the adult qualities of sensitivity, stimulation and autonomy when describing how the adult engaged.
- Think about your setting and consider what you would like to change most about the way the adults engage with children. How could you change this?
- Discuss adult engagement with the staff you work with, share with them the list of things staff found on the Developing Quality through Leadership project. Do they feel they have a voice in your setting? What makes them feel 'inspired' and 'empowered' in your setting?
- Take a moment to consider what you look for in an early years setting, what tells you it is a quality setting? Write down your five key essentials for a high quality setting. Do it individually and then share your lists; can you come up with 'five essentials for a quality setting' as a whole team? Which ones of these are dependent on the quality of the staff?
- If you were to ask parents to consider their 'five essentials for a quality setting' how do you think their list would differ from yours? Send out a questionnaire to parents asking them what they look for in a setting and what they look for in the staff that work with their children.
- Ask the children what they like about the people who look after them? What makes a really good teacher/key person/early years practitioner? What do the children think and what do they want from the staff that care for them?
- If you were to introduce peer observation in your setting what would you personally gain from the process?
- If you were to introduce peer observation in your setting how would your setting benefit? What would be your barriers when introducing it? How will you overcome these?

References

Bertram, A. (1996) Effective early childhood educators: Developing a methodology for improvement. Unpublished thesis. Coventry: Coventry University Available at: https://www.curve.coventry.ac.uk/open/items/ae2a0bef-1f7e-e50e-35a49ca6bccf/1/ (accessed 16 February, 2015).

Bion, W. (nd) Container and contained. Available at: https://www.cpor.org/otc/Bion(1985)Container AndContained.pdf (accessed 1 May, 2015).

DfE (Department for Education) (2012) *Statutory Framework for the Early Years Foundation Stage*. Cheshire: Department for Education.

DfES (Department for Education and Skills) (2002) *Investors in Children Consultation Paper*. Nottingham: Department for Education and Skills.

Formosinho, J. (2003) Childhood pedagogy. The importance of interactions and relations. In Laevers, F. and Heylen, L. (eds) *Involvement of Children and Teacher Style. Insights from an International Study on Experiential Education*. Leuven, Belgium: Leuven University Press, pp. 111–127.

Laevers, F. and Moons, J. (1997) *Enhancing Well-being and Involvement in Children. An Introduction to the Ten Action Points*. Leuven, Belgium: Centre for Experiential Education.

Laevers, F., Bogaerts, M. and Moons, J. (1997) *Experiential Education at Work. A Setting with Five Year Olds*. Manual and videotape. Leuven, Belgium: Centre for Experimental Education.

Mooney, A. (2007) *The Effectiveness of Quality Improvement Programmes for Early Childhood Education and Childcare*. London: Thomas Coram Research Unit.

National Strategies (2007) *Developing Quality through Leadership, Reading. Leading reflective practice through peer observations*. Nottingham: National Strategies.

Office for Standards in Education (Ofsted) (1998) *The Quality of Education in Institutions Inspected under the Nursery Education Funding Arrangements*. London: HMSO.

Office for Standards in Education, Children's Services and Skills (Ofsted) (2014) *Official Statistics Release, Early Years Childcare Inspections and Outcomes*. London: HMSO. Available online at: https://www.gov.uk/government/statistics/official-statistics-early-years-and-childcare-registered-providers-inspections-and-outcomes (accessed 5 February, 2015).

Pascal, C. and Bertram, A. (1997) *Effective Early Learning Project*. Worcester: Centre for Research in Early Childhood.

Pascal, C. and Bertram, A. (2003) *The Effective Early Learning Project. The Quality of Adult Engagement in Early Childhood Settings in the UK*. In Laevers, F. and Heylen, L. (eds) *Involvement of Children and Teacher Style. Insights from an International Study on Experiential Education*. Leuven, Belgium: Leuven University Press, pp. 77–91.

Pascal, C. and Bertram, A. (2005) *Baby Effective Early Learning Project*. Worcester: Amber Publications.

Rogers, C. (1983) *Freedom to Learn for the 80s*. Columbus OH: Charles E. Merill.

Rogoff, B. (1990) *Apprenticeship Thinking. Cognitive Development in Social Context*. Oxford: Oxford University Press.

Sammons, P., Sylva, K., Melhuish, E., Siraj, I., Taggart, B., Smees, R. and Toth, K. (2014) *Influences on Students' Social-Behavioral Development at Age 16. Effective Pre-school, Primary and Secondary Education Project (EPPSE) Research Brief*. London: Institute of Education, Department for Education.

Sylva, K., Melhuish, E., Sammons, P., Siraj-Blatchford, I., Taggart, B. and Elliot, K. (2003) *The Effective Provision of Pre-school Education (EPPE) Project. Findings from the Pre-school Period*. Nottingham: DfES Publications.

Sylva, K., Melhuish, E., Sammons, P., Siraj-Blatchford, I. and Taggart, B. (2004) *The Effective Provision of Pre-school Education (EPPE) Project. Findings from the Primary Years*. Nottingham: DfES Publications.

Sylva, K., Melhuish, E., Sammons, P., Siraj-Blatchford, I. and Taggart, B. (2008) *Final Report from the Primary Phase: Pre-school, School and Family Influences on Children's Development during Key Stage 2 (Age 7–11). The Effective Pre-school and Primary Education 3–11 Project (EPPE3-11)*. Nottingham: DCSF Publications.

Sylva, K., Melhuish, E., Sammons, P., Siraj, I., Taggart, B., Smees, R., Toth, K., Welcomme, W. and Hollingworth, K. (2014) *Students' Educational and Developmental Outcomes at Age 16. Effective Pre-school, Primary and Secondary Education Project (EPPSE) Research Brief*. London: Institute of Education, Department for Education.

Wenger, E. (nd) Communities of practice. A brief introduction. Available at: https://www.wenger-trayner.com (accessed 10 February, 2015).

Wenger, E. (1998) *Communities of Practice. Learning, Meaning and Identity*. Cambridge: Cambridge University Press.

Chapter 6

Embracing levels of involvement

Julie Kent

Embedding wellbeing and involvement in Children's Centre practice

This chapter recounts the journey of one setting, establishing and developing an approach to working with families. The journey can be applied to any early years setting where a team of staff work together to seek to improve the experiences of families in a local community. It highlights the rewards and challenges of working at a micro level with individual families and the dynamic interplay with more macro practice and policy at a national level that has impact on local practice.

As a Centre, our interest in children's involvement and wellbeing came out of our desire to establish a place with high quality provision where parents could not only understand and be involved with their children's learning but also gain insight into how their own levels of wellbeing affected their children's responsiveness and levels of involvement in the short and long term. In a newly established phase two Children's Centre, staff were recruited from a range of backgrounds including Early Years and Childcare, Family Support, Playwork and Health. There was a need, as team leader, to build a shared ethos that encompassed the expectations around providing the Children's Centre core offer, based as it was at the time on the Every Child Matters (2003) outcomes, whilst also meeting the unique needs of the children and families in our community. Our philosophy reflected a UNICEF (2007) statement:

> The true measure of a nation's standing is how well it attends to its children – their health and safety, their maternal security, their education and socialisation and their sense of being loved, valued and included in the families and societies into which they are born

This perspective was the backdrop to the holistic view of the child taken by the staff team as we worked to develop an inclusive and containing environment, characterised by reflective practitioners who were concerned about the impact of adult wellbeing and motivation on the child's level of involvement and wellbeing. As one team member expressed, 'we were concerned about children's wellbeing when they were with us and when they were not with us'. We were also trying to incorporate key Early Years Foundation Stage (EYFS) principles into our setting, bearing in mind that 'good parenting and high quality early learning together provide the foundation children need to make the most of their abilities and talents as they grow up' (DfE, 2014). Reflecting now in hindsight, the relational pedagogical model proposed by Bergum (2003) is one which best embodies the approach taken as we responded to the need to make connections for parents and staff in considering children's learning and development. We saw ourselves as being deeply involved in listening and making connections for and between children, parents, practitioners and the community. Pedagogical leadership needs to involve everyone in the learning process and our view of the child was necessarily reflected in our view of the relationships within the setting, the community and between all parties in the establishing of a new place. 'Rather than viewing leadership practice as a product of a leader's knowledge and skill, the distributed perspective defines it as the interactions between people and their situation' (Spillane, 2005: 143). The learning and development of the staff team went alongside the learning and development of our children and families, and the view that we took of learning was seen throughout the Centre's activity and environment. Papatheodorou and Moyles (2009) also espouse a similar approach in their discussions on pursuing inclusive and dialogic relationships within community settings.

Our services had a focus on the family with a strong emphasis on the very early years, attachment and wellbeing in the ante-natal and post-natal period. With the core offer requiring us to support parenting the Local Authority was, at this point, keen to ensure a county-wide approach to parenting based on the Solihull Parenting Approach (Douglas and Ginty, 2001). All staff were trained in this approach; all Centre services whether in crèches, universal Stay and Play sessions, targeted groups for teenage parents, ante-natal classes or adult learning were to offer a holistic practice.

It was central to our practice that we were mindful of the 'dance of reciprocity' (Brazelton et al., 1974) between adult and child and that contingent responsiveness (Gerhardt, 2004) was modelled and embedded in all Centre work and activity. The centrality of reciprocity from a management perspective was seen in the 'conversations' that were encouraged between team members, partners and parents, as well as with children in the early stages of Centre development. The pedagogical leadership embraced expectancy and an openness to possibilities (Woods, 2013), which meant that the Centre was being built on high quality relationships that recognised the importance of reciprocal communication in supporting and managing change and meeting expectations.

As a result of this, the Centre developed early in its life as a place where parents were supported to become observers of their children as they played and interacted with the environment that was provided; parents were included in our planning for the learning and development of their child. We espoused the view that 'babies learn best by playing with the things they find in their world, and above all by playing with the familiar people who love them' (DfES, 2003: 150). From baby massage to heuristic play sessions, staff modelled and supported parents in 'reading' their baby, to follow their lead and to modify their own language, gaze and 'tone' in response to their child's level of responsiveness. The language of containment and reciprocity (Douglas and Ginty, 2001) provided a lens through which we planned, delivered and reflected upon all Centre activity. Our perspective on containment was based on the work of Bion (1959) and is embodied by an adult who has the insight, understanding and self-efficacy to recognise and bear in mind the anxieties of the child and 'contain' the anxiety with an appropriate and reassuring response that acknowledges the child's stress but does not reinforce it.

A management perspective

It was crucial that all staff shared this ethos, from reception staff and information officers to early years and family support staff, and this informed planning for staff training and supervision within the Centre. It was also significant in the building of an advisory board team where partners, staff and parents all contributed and where all voices were listened to in a professional and reciprocal manner and all contributions were valued. We gathered a group of sensitive yet purposeful adults who were involved in our journey to develop the Centre.

'Effective practice in the early years requires committed, enthusiastic and reflective practitioners with a breadth and depth of knowledge, skills and understanding' (DfES, 2005: 3) and part of the responsibility of management and pedagogical leadership of the team in the establishment of the Centre and its ethos was an investment in training and the development of systems that would facilitate the growth of this type of working, which was grounded in relationships.

It was apparent that support for staff wellbeing was central to developing self-awareness and mindfulness within the team and we worked with an NHS Psychological Wellbeing practitioner to develop staff support and training, as well as to set up parent support around post-natal depression and low mood. A vital factor for consideration here was the need to support staff from different backgrounds through a change of roles and perceptions in a new context. Harris (2004: 402) explores the emotional or 'heart' conditions that are necessary to successfully implement change and she notes that 'a climate of trust .... is essential to foster positive feelings of involvement and ownership'. This would be true for both staff and families. In setting up and leading an early years setting it was essential that there was a connection between our understanding of learning and development and our leadership of the adults in the setting. Andrews (2010: 45) describes this as 'pedagogy based leadership of adults' and notes that if the setting is an emotionally safe place for staff it can also be a safe place within which the child can develop. There are echoes here of the Te Whāriki (1996) curriculum, which Vesty and Wardle explore (Wardle and Vesty, 2014), where wellbeing is encapsulated in the concept of trusting relationships. Trust within the team and between the team and our partners was a high priority as the Centre developed.

From a management perspective, an essential element in developing our parenting groups was to ensure that protected time for practitioner reflection was 'built-in' as part of the group delivery plan. Staff were given time to reflect together following each session. Crucially, this would include not only the staff who delivered the group to parents, but also the staff who had been running the crèche. We were able to note the 'settledness' of the children in the crèche and make connections with the level of mood and anxiety of the parent.

Staff clinical supervision was another central aspect of staff development. Providing staff with a 'secure base' of regular opportunities to reflect and receive mentoring was seen as a way of supporting resilience, self-reliance and personal development, in the same way as a providing a 'secure base' for the child will support exploration. Laevers (2002) sees a child's level of involvement as an indicator of deep level learning, which is linked to a sense of wellbeing in the environment, and, through supporting staff to feel secure, there was a clear hope that this would lead to increased creativity, motivation and working in a focused way. Andrews (2010: 53) expresses this in relation to the EYFS principles, showing how the themes can be used to inform leadership of teams as well as planning outcomes for children; therefore, if as managers we accept that 'people learn to be strong and independent from a base of secure relationships' (ibid.), we need to ensure that staff wellbeing is supported. As part of this supervision we commissioned work with an NHS Psychological Wellbeing practitioner who was able to offer training for staff in mindfulness as well as providing one-to-one supervision to the team, including the team leader. This supervision and training provided the opportunity to consider how mindfulness in the adult is a reflection of intense involvement in the child; staff were able to experience concentration without distraction, which led to energy, creativity and deep level learning in their practice.

The journey with parents

An early group that we ran at the Centre prior to our encounter with the work of Laevers and that embodied the beginnings of our approach to involvement was our heuristic play group. Here, parents were given 'permission', support and encouragement to observe their child as they responded to the resources provided. Children were free to explore, to play with things in their own way and parents could 'stand aside for a while' as Malaguzzi (Edwards *et al.*, 1998) exhorted. In these sessions parents were supported to observe the characteristics of effective learning – playing and exploring, active learning and creating and thinking critically (DfE, 2014) – displayed by their children and echoed in the descriptors from the Leuven Scales: fascination, concentration, persistence and motivation (Laevers, 1994). Out of these experiences both parents and staff were able to recognise how a child's level of involvement is not fixed but will ebb and flow in response to a range of elements both within and without the child and, on reflection, it is possible to see the roots of our interest in the work of Laevers beginning to develop from this point.

Encounter with staff: 1

Retrospective discussion with staff involved in the early implementation of the Children's Centre offer shows the threads beginning to develop as to how directing parents to support their children's learning and involvement had to become intentional in our thinking and planning. An early years professional reflected: 'were parents really interested in their children's learning or was the Centre viewed just as a safe place to play'? We reminisced on how we were aware that parents' perceptions of their own competence was sometimes poor once their children moved beyond babyhood and that there was a sense of 'waiting' for formal education to start, with many parents expressing the view that their child was 'bored' at home and 'ready for nursery'. We recognised that 'there is an ongoing judgement to be made by practitioners about the balance between activities led by children, and activities led or guided by adults' (DfE, 2014). We reflected on how the environment was a positive place with planned areas and thought-out opportunities for socialisation but also how we had to gently introduce parents to a deeper engagement with their children's learning through 'sharing our observations with them, suggesting small thinking points, putting information on our display boards and showing consistency (in our own approaches)'. Our Centre statement encouraged parents to allow exploration by highlighting in group publicity that children might get messy and that it did not matter! 'We were also trying to break the mould of parent perceptions of what a Stay and Play session was and that it was not about parents sitting and drinking tea and children doing whatever they liked. But we still wanted the environment to be welcoming and non-judgemental; there was a balance for us between "interfering" and engagement. We wanted to show parents that it was okay to watch their children playing'. This was clearly developed through our heuristic play sessions where children were allowed to explore the materials as they were interested in them and parents were encouraged not to direct their children's play but instead to observe their children and to allow the play to develop and reach a natural finishing point without an adult lead.

Staff recalled, 'parents asked us to do it again! They became much more open-minded to their child's learning and talked about how they adapted to their children's interests and involvement'.

We wanted parents to experience an environment where play is seen as an end in itself and is valued as meaningful for the child (Te Whāriki, 1996). From a management perspective, it was essential to develop a knowledgeable staff team who could understand both children and parents, who could run our open 'universal' sessions as well as supporting the planning and leading of more targeted small groups with a parenting focus and enable parents to access these. The balance between providing childcare, early education and family support as expected in the Children's Centre core offer was challenging but the relational pedagogy (Bergum, 2003) was the structure through which this holistic offer was developed and shaped. It was especially important to consider that the involvement and wellbeing levels of practitioners would affect the wellbeing of the children and families who we were engaging with. Bradford (2012) cites research by Walsh and Gardner (2005) where the levels of motivation of adults had a clear impact on the involvement of children. Because we knew there was a clear correlation between adult motivation and the child's level of involvement we worked hard on our own language, communication, planning and supervision to promote an effective environment where staff also felt contained.

It was at this point that staff also became involved with the Northamptonshire Baby Room Project©. In training and dialogue with highly specialist practitioners we were strongly supported to recognise that 'babies do not usually come into this world as relaxed, contented little individuals. They are full of turbulent, powerful feelings, often associated with physical sensations that they need parents to help them deal with' (Solihull Approach resource pack, 2006). We began to recognise and help parents to recognise that children have intense emotions and experiences, and to embrace the importance of being 'in step' with their child in order to support their wellbeing. In particular, we created an environment where parents and practitioners were able to respond sensitively to babies' low involvement or wellbeing as well as sharing their curiosity in times of high involvement. Through our participation in the training and delivery of 'Baby Room' sessions for our parents we engaged with close observations of the babies' interests and as practitioners we were able also to observe high degrees of sustained shared thinking (Sylva et al., 2004) between parents and their babies. We experienced fascination and amazement as we learned about baby brain development from enthusiastic, reflective and insightful practitioners and this was reflected in displays, photographs and 'thinking points', which we displayed across the Centre, including on the back of the toilet door! The signs of wellbeing were clearly present in the openness and receptivity of all involved in this project (Laevers, 2002).

Using the Leuven Scales of wellbeing and involvement

Alongside our Centre, at a neighbouring Centre in our cluster, staff teams had already embedded their approach to supporting children and families through their engagement with the Leuven Scales (Laevers, 1994) for involvement and wellbeing. Similar themes were developed as staff embraced this approach in their work, using the scales and the concepts within them as a tool to support their understanding and evaluation of the learning and development of children accessing Centre services. Significantly, in relation to the Centre remit around family support, the observations of children were used with parents attending Centre groups as part of the intervention for the whole family, enabling parents to understand their children's behaviour in a new way. This understanding was threaded into supporting parents and staff to identify schemas and patterns within the child's play (Arnold, 2003).

Encounter with staff: 2

An early years worker reported how a parent was frustrated with her child's behaviour in one of the Centre groups and 'struggled to see how (her child) was highly involved in tipping out resources from the toy baskets around the setting'. Once this was put into the context of his 'scattering' schema the parent was able to view his behaviour in a completely different light. The worker describes how, as a result of using the Leuven Scales, Centre staff were able to support parents in understanding the process of their children's learning and in providing a containing environment that enhanced wellbeing and responded to the child's level of involvement.

> It's been great for me sharing my knowledge with parents and it has increased my confidence as a practitioner. I have seen how through identifying and monitoring child wellbeing we are able to empower parents and help them to identify their own wellbeing and its impact on the family. We make a link between the child's emotions and their play and behaviour and help parents to develop 'encouraging' as opposed to 'discouraging' behaviours themselves. Involvement is difficult to quantify and explain but once they've (the parents) got it they can see it and it can really change the relationships (between parent and child). We show the parents that involvement takes energy and concentration, which can lead to tiredness and (apparent) behaviour difficulties. We encourage (the parents) to make links with how *they* feel and to put themselves in their child's shoes. (In the Centre) levels of wellbeing and involvement are part of everyday practice and I am embarrassed that I (previously) had not thought more deeply about this.

The observation and assessment of child wellbeing and involvement clearly 'clicked' with passionate practitioners who appreciated that the children they are working with do not come on their own. Through the dual foci of Children's Centres on family support and parenting we started to understand the subtle interactions between levels of involvement and responsiveness and its impact on mood, behaviour and interaction (Manning-Morton, 2014). We saw our role as one to support parents to recognise and respond to children's self-expression, to identify their children's involvement, to value the process of play and to 'caption' this in the Centre learning journeys that parents completed with support from Centre staff. As Bradford (2012: 43) states:

> in Early Years ... a team is a group of people who work together to meet the aims of the establishment or setting ... professionals working in the field of Early Years, therefore, need to be skilled in, and to understand the nature of, collaborative practice ... Early years work is people-based, highly dependent on inter-personal relationships and shared values.

Our application of the EYFS (DfE, 2014) within Centre planning was informed by this 'lens' of wellbeing and involvement through which we were able to view the learning and development of children in the setting. It was easier to see how to work with the whole child in the context of their daily experiences when we did not just focus on outcomes and 'levels' but used this lens to enhance our perspective of the unique child.

Encounter with staff: 3

Staff from the neighbouring Centre describe how they used the Leuven Scales of wellbeing specifically in the targeted Solihull Parenting and 'Little Thinkers' groups and used the levels of involvement in other universal sessions as 'a way of helping parents to see how wellbeing affected involvement and then had an impact on behaviour'. Staff commented particularly on the insights that they were able to nurture in parents when considering how their children felt and how this was evidenced in their levels of involvement.

One practitioner commented on the 'lightbulb moment when a father commented that he had always thought that children were happy all the time. It really helped parents to understand that their child's behaviour was a reflection of their wellbeing and the levels of involvement were evidence of this which we could share with them.'

Staff explain how their whole team approach has links to the Parents Involved in their Children's Learning (PICL) approach (Pen Green team based in Corby, Northants) and how their observations are written up using photo sequences, EYFS areas of learning, the Leuven Scales and any evidence of a child's interest in play or schemas. They particularly stress the way that the concept of involvement is threaded throughout Centre planning, activity and display, with narratives attached to photo display boards that capture the theme of involvement and use the language of involvement to caption, describe and interpret children's levels of involvement. 'It is routine for staff to role model the language of feelings and

(Continued)

(Continued)

involvement as we talk to children and parents, naming emotions and helping parents to see that it is normal for their child's mood and involvement levels to vary and, in fact, that to sustain high levels of involvement over a long period is tiring and not always sustainable'. This understanding is also shared with other professionals in family meetings and case conferences, challenging perceptions of children as 'only' being a child and not likely to be affected by the emotional climate around them.

Key to this way of working can be seen to be the understanding of a pedagogical approach that is applied across all aspects of practice, relationships and learning within the setting.

Children's Centre Core Purpose

At this point in our journey, however, the Children's Centres became subject to new guidance and legislation around the parameters of our role with the implementation of the new Children's Centre Core Purpose by the coalition government in 2012. This presented a challenge to how we would be able to continue to work within the ethos or pedagogy that we had been developing over the previous four years. It specifically stated that the focus of the work was to be targeted towards 'those in most need' and we started to consider how this would be worked out in the ongoing running of Centre services and continued building of supportive relationships within the community served by the Centres. We had always worked with all children and families in our reach areas but the increased focus on targeted working with the most vulnerable of these families made it even more important to maintain our ethos of providing a high quality learning environment for children and those parents who we were supporting to re-engage with learning. We saw that these were the families where adult mood, wellbeing and levels of stress were having the most profound impact on the wellbeing and development of children both in the short and long term. Coming from a health background it was possible to make connections with research in this area to verbalise the challenge ahead:

> Relationships, too, are never smooth, and the harder ones teach us even more about ourselves as well as about others. Perhaps it is the difficult patients, says Liaschenko (1994), who need most respect and work: a participant in her study says: 'It's those hard ones that really need a conscious effort at respect, a conscious effort of taking the time, a conscious effort to figure out how – if you can make a connection with them, how you can do it and sometimes you can't' (p. 88). We must not give up too soon. How can we persevere? How can we find the time or more significantly how can we create the space that is needed for relationships to develop?
>
> (Bergum, 2003: 125)

The wellbeing and involvement lens clearly encouraged us to use our understanding to maintain our focus on the fundamental importance of early relationships to the wellbeing and safety of the child. Viewed through this lens our remit to continue to support parents to look at things through a child's eyes in their relationships with the child fitted well with the need to support our most vulnerable families; from a management perspective, however, we were aware that as one parent expressed to us, 'it will not be the same' and the need within the changing climate to manage the expectations of both families and staff became an overwhelming element of the role. We were moving from having built up relationships with families through universal services to a more targeted approach that was based much more on time-limited interventions, and our relational approach was consequently compromised.

Andrews (2010: 46) notes how, in Children's Centres, the 'energy of development' may be followed by 'the concerns of consolidation and sustainability' and these issues were at the forefront of Local Authority decision-making at this time; consequently their priorities were changing too. The need to ensure children were at a level of 'school readiness' seemed to disregard the significance of the present moment and the positive outcomes that our families were already experiencing as a result of their 'participation' – reduced isolation, an increase in prosocial behaviour, a reduction in defensiveness and an increased openness in response to the non-judgemental environment at the Centre. The fact that parents and children were not stigmatised was, in fact, beginning to build 'community' and the concern was that the 'time' element of our enabling environment was going to be eroded (Early Education, 2012). As Woods and Wardle (2013: 113) note, 'an enabling environment allows babies and young children *time* to explore just as adults need time to adjust to new ways of working'. Initially, we had been able to shape our services and develop our roles, working innovatively and flexibly in response to the needs of our own families and community. We had recognised that 'people develop and learn in different ways and at different rates' (Andrews, 2010: 53) but now our work was being much more channelled in a specific direction with boundaries being changed, and yet we needed to maintain an awareness that our anxiety about change did not affect our focus on the needs of children and families. Andrews (ibid.: 63) notes how important it is that 'the staff team becomes resilient and able to understand and model the holding and containing of change anxieties in others'. Self-regulation in leadership was essential at this stage – one had to be sure of one's own core values as well as being empathic towards the feelings of others (Manning-Morton, 2014).

We were working with those families where we knew that the wellbeing of the parent had a significant effect on the wellbeing of the child, as already noted earlier in this chapter. Whereas secure parents 'relate with their infant as if the child had a mind and what goes on in that mind is worth knowing' (Fonagy, 2000 cited in Howe, 2005: 19), we knew that many of our parents were preoccupied with their own needs and, in fact, many sought to meet their own emotional needs through the parent–child relationship, having great difficulty in seeing the world from the child's perspective. These were the parents who were rigid and inflexible (Howe, 2005: 10) in interpreting their child's behaviours with a limited view of the possibilities, in particular when making judgements about how their child was feeling, often misinterpreting the signs such that tired, poorly, hungry, sick or distressed babies were described as being naughty or annoying: 'He's doing my head in.' 'She doesn't like me.' 'She's doing it on purpose because she knows how to press my buttons.'

Anecdotally we had been aware that children in a crèche for a parenting support group appeared often unsettled or fractious; and, as we reflected in a more purposeful way, it was clear that our evidence could be corroborated by research such as that cited by Gerhardt (2004) who observed that babies with less sensitive mothers exhibited more irritability, but when parents were supported to recognise their babies' signals and respond appropriately there was an improvement in the relationship. Our role was to help parents to reflect on their own emotional state as well as on their child's so that there was a level of attunement. We believed that 'more positive emotions .... help children approach and persist with activities that help in their exploration of the world' and that 'joy encourages us to relax, play, learn and approach others', reflecting the view of Laevers that children with good wellbeing will show persistence, involve themselves for longer in activity and be more contented.

This linked well to the Solihull perspective that we held around containment and being able to 'contain' a distressed child; for parents who themselves are 'uncontained', when 'faced with a needy, vulnerable or distressed child the ... parent feels disorganised, out of control and without a strategy to deal with [his] own emotional arousal or that of [his] child' (Howe, 2005: 39). Team reflection and planning, including discussion with our parent forum and advisory board enabled us to revise and adapt our services with families in mind. It must be noted, however, that many families did experience a sense of anxiety during this period of change, feeling 'dejected, sad, frightened or angry' (Laevers, 1994), all of which we were able to observe during this time. Here, alongside our understanding of involvement, we were having to engage with concepts of resilience in the face of change. It was clear that, as a pedagogical leader, planning and provision for our own wellbeing and that of our families would have to be a high priority and that no-one else would do that for us.

Reflecting back 18 months later with the wellbeing practitioner at 'one step removed' from the situation, it is easier to see what was happening and how our focus on wellbeing and mindfulness had been instrumental in developing resilience within the team.

Encounter with staff: 4

As a Psychological Wellbeing Practitioner (PWP), my role at the Children's Centre (CC) was to provide information, supervision and training to Centre staff and parents based on my knowledge of the development, identification and treatment of common mental health disorders such as depression, anxiety disorders and stress, using evidence-based treatments including Psychoeducation, Cognitive Behavioural Therapy (CBT) and Mindfulness.

It is recognised that wellbeing, physical and mental health impacts not just on our own day-to-day life but also directly impacts on the wellbeing, physical and mental health of our family, friends and colleagues. Thus, improvements experienced by CC staff and parents will directly benefit the health, wellbeing and development of the children who attend the Centre and their siblings.

CBT and Psychoeducation enable people to gain an understanding of how stress and distress affects how we think, behave and feel; how strategies can be developed to break into this 'vicious cycle' and improve health and wellbeing. Mindfulness practice facilitates self-awareness, acceptance and self-compassion.

Staff training was 'protected time' and delivered to all team members, clerical and clinical, away from the distractions of their usual place of work. Training, individual and group supervision were available for all staff including the CC manager. Supervision encompassed personal and professional matters, an opportunity to share in a 'safe' environment and problem-solve options to overcome difficulties. Supervision was also available for Peer Supporters, an opportunity to reflect on the sessions they had supported and their own needs.

The training provided the staff with a number of opportunities:

- to explore their own wellbeing and stress management strategies;
- to recognise stress and distress in themselves and others;
- to gain greater insight into the links between thoughts/physical feelings/mood and behaviours;
- to recognise that making small changes can improve wellbeing, mental and physical health;
- to develop self-care strategies including mindfulness;
- to be able to share their personal experiences of the benefits of therapeutic approaches with parents;
- increased knowledge of the approaches that would be offered;
- increased confidence in recognising people who would benefit from interventions.

A group aimed at parents who were experiencing low mood, post-natal depression, stress or anxiety, was developed collaboratively between the PWP and CC staff. Each session had a wellbeing theme including mood and food, stress and relaxation, relationships, self-care and self-esteem. Close proximity of the group room to the crèche enabled parents to see their child if needed, while having 'protected' time to have some of their own needs met.

Sessions ended with participants planning a realistic and achievable activity to do the following week, guided by the week's topic, and that would enhance their wellbeing, build resilience and enable the participant to generalise strategies into day-to-day life.

The Warwick–Edinburgh Mental Well-Being Scale (WEMWBS) and an evaluation form were used in the first and last sessions to measure outcomes and facilitate further development of the group. The WEMWBS demonstrated improvements in the wellbeing scores or all but one participant, including CC staff. The evaluation form highlighted learning about wellbeing and emotions, and recognition that participants were not alone and that they could help each other. Participants also recorded increased confidence and several wanted to help in a Peer Support role; sadly this opportunity was lost when the CC closed and the groups ended.

As we reviewed our work together, we noted that mindfulness was the ultimate level of involvement and that, in using mindfulness ourselves and supporting our parents to become 'mindful', we had been using concepts that bore a strong relationship to Laevers' approach and this had enabled us to offer a holistic service across the Centre.

We continued for a further 18 months with our adapted service, in particular embracing the new shared working agreements established with the troubled families' teams and working to link our services more with theirs through referral systems and information sharing. Any setting is part of a wider ecological system (Bronfenbrenner, 1979) and this was a particularly relevant consideration in leadership of Children's Centres, but is true of every early years setting if it seeks to meet the needs of children in the wider context of their families and communities. Surrounding the work developed to meet the needs of its own community, there will always be a wider 'macro' context in which services are placed and that will inform, direct and shape service delivery to a greater or lesser extent. For the Children's Centres, this context had always been the economic and political agenda around the Children's Centre Core Purpose.

The end of one journey and the trails for new ones to be taken

Unfortunately for our community, our families, our staff and our partners, the model of Children's Centre provision that had been developed in our reach area became incompatible with changing Government and Local Authority priorities around Children's Centre delivery, and the Centre, as it was, closed in 2014 with services being distributed elsewhere to alternative providers. Reflections on our journey still feel difficult. This was change on a large scale, the result of determinants from the macro system outside of our influence and beyond our control; for an organisation that had sought to embrace change while maintaining a containing environment, the change was a shock but one that had to be accepted. Covey (2004) in his discussion on change and influence notes that some things, although in our 'circle of concern', may not be within our 'circle of influence', and this is something with which many of us are still grappling. Having experienced the 'mourning' stage of team development, and in the absence of the containing environment, many of us have had to be 'self-contained' and continue to take responsibility for our own learning and development. Some staff now work in new and different roles in schools and other settings, and encouragement can be found in the thought that their adaptability, resilience and experience developed within the Children's Centre is now being worked out and demonstrated in their practice in these places. As leaders, some of us are now involved in the teaching and development of students and we hope that they will become practitioners who will reflect on their own wellbeing and what this brings to their practice, as well as considering the wellbeing of the child. Professional development, begun in an early years setting, will continue to be worked out in the development of future practitioners who benefit significantly from being taught by practitioners with recent, relevant and reflective experience. It does seem that once Laevers' involvement tools are assimilated, both observing and involving children, as well as students and staff teams, will always be part of a 'toolbox' for reflecting upon and evaluating provision. Laevers, in a keynote speech, 2009, said: 'The job by the way that will never end.'

Learning will continue to happen but this may not be the optimum experience of all those involved in this Centre's life, in particular our children and families whose journey has not ended at a destination that they might have chosen. The hope of practitioners is that we might have supported a number of families in the community to develop resilience and insight into their own levels of wellbeing, which will enhance their levels of involvement with their children's learning, their own development and the needs of their community, and afford them a 'reservoir in times of drought'. (Bruce, 2005)

Provocations

- How aware are you of the potential impact of parental wellbeing and involvement on the learning and development of children in your setting? In what ways could you use this information?
- How could you develop the fascination and curiosity of an observer in your staff and parents?
- Through what lens do you and your team view the learning and development of the child?
- Consider how you use the pedagogical leadership approach as a tool for staff to develop and reflect on their own practice. Think about how to build in learning experiences for staff that echo what we want them to provide for children.
- As a manager, what is your role in acting as a 'container' for the wellbeing needs of your team and how do you maintain your own containment?

References

Andrews, M. (2010) Managing change and pedagogical leadership. In Robins, A. and Callan, S. (eds) *Managing Early years Settings*. London: Sage, pp. 45–64.

Arnold, C. (2003) *Observing Harry*. Maidenhead: Open University Press.

Bergum, V. (2003) Relational pedagogy. Embodiment, improvisation, and interdependence. *Nursing Philosophy*, 4(2): 121–128.

Bion, W. (1959) *Second Thoughts*. London: Karnac.

Bradford, H. (2012) *The Wellbeing of Children under Three*. London: David Fulton.

Brazelton, T., Koslowski, B. and Main, M. (1974) The origins of reciprocity. The early mother–infant interaction. In Lewis, M. and Rosenblum, L. A. (eds) *The Effect of the Infant on Its Caregiver*. New York: Wiley, pp. 49–76.

Bronfenbrenner, U. (1979) *The Ecology of Human Development. Experiments by Nature and Design*. Cambridge, MA: Harvard University Press.

Bruce, T. (2005) *Early Childhood Education*. 3rd edn. London: Hodder Arnold.

Covey, S. R. (2004) *The Seven Habits of Highly Effective People*. Reprinted edn. New York: Simon & Schuster.

DfE (Department for Education) (2014). *Statutory Framework for the Early Years Foundation Stage*. Available at: https://www.gov.uk/government/uploads/system/uploads/attachment_data/file/335504/EYFS_framework_from_1_September_2014__with_clarification_note.pdf (accessed 4 May, 2015).

DfES (Department for Education and Skills) (2003) *Birth to Three Matters. A Framework to Support Children in their Earliest Years*. DfES Publishing: Nottingham.

DfES (Department for Education and Skills) (2005) *Key Elements of Effective Practice*. Norwich: HMSO.

Douglas, H. and Ginty, M. (2001) The Solihull approach. Changes in health visiting practice. *Community Practitioner*, 74(6): 222–224.

Early Education (2012) *Development Matters in the Early Years Foundation Stage (EYFS)*. London: Early Education.

Edwards, C., Gandini, L. and Forman, G. (eds) (1998) *The Hundred Languages of Children. The Reggio Emilia Approach – Advanced Reflections*. 2nd edn. Westport, CT: Ablex Publishing.

Every Child Matters (2003) Available at: https://www.education.gov.uk/consultations/downloadable Docs/EveryChildMatters.pdf (accessed 16 May, 2015).

Gerhardt, S. (2004) *Why Love Matters. How Affection Shapes a Baby's Brain*. London: Routledge.

Harris, B. (2004) Leading by Heart. *School Leadership and Management*, 24(4): 391–404.

Howe, D. (2005) *Child Abuse and Neglect. Attachment, Development and Intervention*. London: Palgrave-Macmillan.

Laevers, F. (ed.) (1994) *The Leuven Involvement Scale for Young Children, LIS-YC.* Manual. Leuven, Belgium: Centre for Experiential Education.

Laevers, F (2002) *Research on Experiential Education. A Selection of Articles.* Leuven, Belgium: Centre for Experiential Education.

Laevers, F. (2009) Interview with Ferre Laevers from the Scottish Learning Festival. Available at: http://www.educationscotland.gov.uk/video/f/video tcm4565868.asp (accessed 14 September, 2014).

Manning-Morton, J. (2014) *Exploring Wellbeing in the Early Years.* Maidenhead: Open University Press.

Ministry of Education (1996) *Te Whāriki.* Wellington, New Zealand: Learning Media.

Papatheodorou, T. and Moyles, J. (eds) (2009) *Cross-cultural Perspectives on Early Childhood.* London: Sage.

Solihull Approach Resource Pack © (2006) Solihull NHS Care Trust.

Spillane, J. P. (2005). Distributive leadership. *The Educational Forum*, 69(2): 143–150.

Sylva, K., Mulhuish, E., Sammons, P., Siraj-Blatchfors, I. and Taggart, B. (2004) *The Effective Provision of Pre-school Education (EPPE) Project: Findings from the Primary Years.* Nottingham: Department for Education and Science.

UNICEF (2007) *Child Poverty in Perspective. An Overview of Child Wellbeing in Rich Countries.* Report card 7. Florence: UNICEF Innocenti Research Centre.

Wardle, L. and Vesty, S. (2014) Exploring children's wellbeing and motivations. In Woods, A. (ed.) *The Characteristics of Effective Learning. Creating and Capturing the Possibilities in the Early Years.* London: Routledge, pp. 23–38.

Woods, A. (ed.) (2013) *Child-initiated Play and Learning. Planning for Possibilities in the Early Years.* London: Routledge.

Woods, A. and Wardle, L. (2013) Leading possibilities. In Woods, A. (ed.) *Child-initiated Play and Learning. Planning for Possibilities in the Early Years.* London: Routledge, Chapter 8.

Chapter 7

Nurturing involvement through assessment and planning for possibilities

Catherine Gripton

Nurturing children's involvement with their play is an essential aspect of facilitating learning for young children. Involvement is important for developing concentration, engaging with deeper learning, enabling higher order thinking, building connections, supporting well-being, promoting independence and creating a truly *learning environment* for all children. There are many ways in which practitioners, families and peers support a child's involvement. Through careful assessment and planning, practitioners can significantly support children in becoming more involved with their play thus enabling deeper learning.

This book seeks to explore how Laevers' work on nurturing involvement is underpinned by research and theory, informs current practice and can shape our future practice. In Chapter 1, Woods considered why involvement is important within educational practice, exploring the theoretical framework within which involvement exists, and established that involvement is about the quality of human activity. She explained that together, well-being and involvement are a measure of deep learning through the developmental changes (accommodation) that they indicate. Within Chapter 2 she takes this further through explaining how useable and useful the levels are in focusing practitioner's thinking and reflection, indeed in defining practice. She provides examples of how using the levels of well-being and involvement can support practitioners in effectively supporting children to progress in learning in the longer term through identification and intervention to support the whole child.

The first two chapters provide a landscape within which the following chapters sit. These later chapters explore how involvement and well-being can be nurtured through provision within the indoor and outdoor learning environment. They explore the vital role of the adult in nurturing children's involvement through assessment, planning and interaction and through working with parents and leading groups of practitioners to effectively support this. In Chapter 3, Brown explains the vital importance of the environment in nurturing involvement and explores how environments that are deemed 'stimulating' can both foster and inhibit children's involvement. Moran, through Chapter 4, develops this further through her exploration of the outdoor learning environment, systematically considering all aspects of what is needed to support involvement and how the outdoors affords all of these possibilities to children with particularly high levels of satisfaction experienced by children. She argues that the constantly changing outdoor environment affords rich possibilities for deep learning and many surprises, which we, as practitioners, embrace in order for children to become highly involved. Moran, in dialogue with practitioners from two settings, explores how practice in the outdoors can be developed to more effectively nurture children's involvement, through investigating how individual children engaged in deep learning, indicated through high levels of involvement and well-being.

In Chapter 5, McEwan provides an additional dimension by exploring the role of adults in nurturing involvement. She argues that warmth is key and that sensitivity, stimulation and providing autonomy are crucial and long lasting. She goes on to explain how peer practitioner observation can effectively be used to enhance the quality of adult engagement and sets out guidance for establishing a shared approach to introducing peer observations within a setting. Kent, in Chapter 6, contextualises the importance of practitioners' well-being in developing dispositions for learning through involvement and additionally highlights the central importance of parents' well-being and the impact this has upon the child's involvement. She considers how deliberately and overtly supporting parents to observe their children, to value their activity and to support their child's involvement makes a profound difference to young children's learning and development. The role of the practitioner is again explored within this chapter in terms of how we nurture children's possibilities through our assessment and planning.

Observing involvement is intensely human. It requires a human connection between observer and observed. To interpret the facial expressions and eye movement described in the LIS-YC signals of involvement (Laevers, 1994), requires empathetic interpretation. We draw upon our shared experiences with the child as well as our life experience to enable us as practitioners to make authentic and meaningful sense of what we see. This raises questions regarding how we engage with improving practice. It implies that we can learn little about the quality of educational provision by observing empty environments. This seems somewhat obvious; however, this also suggests that two very similar settings may be of very different quality, which challenges our notions of best practice. Excellent practice therefore resides within our ability to nurture specific children's possibilities through provision, which enables and supports them as individuals to experience sustained well-being and involvement, and which recognises and then adapts provision specifically for them as they develop and learn.

As the quality of a setting is determined by the interplay between each specific group of children and their environment, the quality of the education can vary even when the setting is relatively consistent owing to the changing needs, interests and capabilities of the children, which are in constant flux, even when the group of children remains constant. This has considerable implications for curriculum, accountability, quality assurance and improvement of educational settings. Where effectiveness is measured and developed through indicators of learning, such as levels of well-being and involvement, deeper and more sustained learning will occur. External ideas from training or literature, uniform expectations of physical environments or timetables, inflexible measurement tools or checks and restrictive curriculum and assessment requirements could inhibit the very rapid, deep and lifelong learning they aim to promote. This requires a long-term view with a *process*-orientated emphasis, which can be difficult to champion within a culture of short-term, outcome-related performance measures. As practitioners and early years leaders our influence here is, however, significant. We support children to learn deeply through creating powerful learning environments, engaging with deep professional development, being energetic involved adults, having a process-orientated approach and observing for involvement and well-being. This demands so much more from us than statutory curriculum and assessment (Laevers, 2005a).

Practitioners support children's learning through their involvement and their pedagogy. Utilising levels of involvement to improve effectiveness occurs within a real 'field of action' with all of its real-world restrictions and limitations (Laevers, 2000: 28). Improvements can be made to support higher levels of involvement on the smallest of scales, which have a significant impact upon deepening learning (Laevers, 2002). Indeed, the very human nature of involvement is a deeply optimistic notion. It empowers us as practitioners that we are all innately equipped with the ability to observe involvement and therefore able to make changes to provision to better support our children's involvement and therefore learning. It is through practising, experience and training that we can draw out and fine tune these skills but they are nevertheless within us all.

The central argument of this book is that nurturing involvement is central to the learning and development of young children. Within everyday practice, levels of involvement are evident in children's experiences and are nurtured by practitioners, as well as families and other children, in a myriad of ways. This vital element of our work with children is recognised and valued within this chapter as I draw upon understanding of involvement as inherent within all aspects of learning and therefore key for nurturing possibilities in children's learning. In considering assessment and planning, we draw and build upon the theoretical underpinning and grounded practice that is explained in preceding chapters and consider how we as practitioners can assess and plan in order to nurture children's involvement and engage them in deep learning.

Assessing process

Laevers (2002: 9) challenges an 'overreliance on educational outcomes'. This book invites us as practitioners to recognise and expect children to follow possibilities without anticipation of outcome, resolution or goal in terms of product or conclusion, a key argument being that we should view involvement as within a process whereby a final outcome is usually not known and actually not desirable. This point is illustrated by an encounter with Jemma who is listening to music but journeys through several stages to creating a curtain for a theatre. She makes decisions along the way and there are many possible end products that are considered, some tangible and some imagined. Each change of direction is purposeful and considered. She is not losing concentration by leaving some ideas behind; her leaving them behind is evidence of increased concentration and involvement.

Encounter: Jemma and Ma Baker

Six-year-old Jemma and eight-year-old Nicole are listening to the Boney M song 'Ma Baker' whilst playing.

Jemma sings along and then tells Nicole, 'I think Ma Baker wears a black, a black sort of suit'.

'Do you think she wears glasses?' (Nicole wears glasses).

(Continued)

(Continued)

Jemma leaves the room and returns moments later with some paper and felt pens and draws a picture of a person with grey shoes, black suit and earrings, blue necklace, pink bag and wearing glasses. She leaves the room again returning with scissors and cuts a strip from the bottom of the paper, cutting the shoes off, pauses, then cuts around the figure saying, 'we could make a puppet show'.

Jemma leaves the room again and returning to Mum asks if there is any black paper as they have run out of white. Mum fetches a pile of white paper and gives some sheets to Jemma. Jemma counts the pages and tells Mum that she has given her an odd number of pages. Mum gives her one more page. Nicole and Jemma spread the pages out in two rows of three and cut sticky tape to stick the pages together. Jemma leaves the room and returns with several rolls of wrapping paper. Pulling the wrapping paper from one of the rolls, she finds there is very little left but has an idea for the cardboard tube, which she asks Nicole to help her stick to the papers.

Nicole finds it difficult to cut the tape as Jemma holds it. Jemma suggest she 'goes to the back of it', Nicole frowns and says, 'you do it'. They swap over, Jemma cuts the tape and sticks the tube to the pages.

When the tube is stuck on by several pieces of tape, Jemma holds the tube and waves the pages exclaiming, 'it's like sailing the boat!'

Nicole lifts up a new roll of wrapping paper and Jemma tells her, 'Mum won't let us open that one, that's new … can we open this one Mummy? Cos it's Ma Baker. 'Thanks Mum' she says as Mum agrees.

Jemma turns the tube and sheets over so the tape is on the underside, 'we need wrapping paper for the drawers!' She cuts out wrapping paper for curtains (one piece). Nicole suggests that the smaller piece of wrapping paper goes along the bottom of the sheets and Jemma agrees enthusiastically saying, 'it can be like the dance floor'.

Jemma mimes how to open curtains and tells Nicole that needs to say, 'wooow, welcome to the stage'. She leaves and returns with a strip of stickers and asks who is doing the show, writes a sticker for each person (some are not actually there).

Jemma picks up her Ma Baker puppet and says, 'she wants people to know that she is a baddy'; Nicole is indignant, 'no she doesn't'.

Jemma says, 'gimme all your money', mimicking the voice from the song. Jemma says, 'pretend there is like, um …, like a school going to the theatre and we could have some food with them in a café or outside'. Nicole agrees and they play the song again.

Jemma continues on her own as Nicole is colouring her own Ma Baker picture. She moves the pages and tube and arranges the wrapping paper on top of them. 'This is the tricky bit,' she says, as she cuts a small triangle out of wrapping paper. 'I need to cut a hole in it like on your curtains (to Mum) but it's tricky.'

Mum offers to cut the hole, Jemma asks her to make the hole bigger as 'it needs to be big enough for the pole to fit through'. Mum asks if the hole is okay and Jemma slides the triangle onto the tube and says that it is but that they are going to need quite a few more.

Jemma cuts several similar pieces, cutting out the hole for herself this time and slides two more onto the tube. She sticks the pieces with holes to the wrapping paper curtain. 'I need to stick them so they don't slide off … I will sort that later.'

She cuts the wrapping paper curtain in half to make two curtains where there was one before, asking Nicole, who has finished her picture and shown it to Jemma, to help her cut the tape. She leaves the project and the Ma Baker puppet at this point and moves on to a different activity. Mum later asks her if she wants the puppet and curtains keeping and Gemma replies, 'Na!'

In the encounter, Jemma does not create a theatre, story or role-play. Jemma is content to have explored and engaged with each element within her process and to have experienced 'flow' (Csíkszentmihályi, 2002) and is therefore ultimately satisfied. In this way a high level of involvement is not a peak but a journey through a series of peaks, challenges and other experiences. Dewey (1910: 40) likens this move to a 'unified conclusion' to a ship staying on course through constantly moving. For Jemma, her engagement with creative thinking is paramount, she does not view her efforts as unfinished in anyway (Craft, 2002) and has achieved balance between the known and the new. This raises questions for us as practitioners around when an activity is truly 'finished' and how we know that it is. Do we look for indicators of a child's satisfaction when they choose to move away physically and emotionally, or when there is sufficient external evidence that it has occurred? This also suggests that an adult model of task planning, executing and completion could mislead us in assessing young children's learning.

In the encounter with Jemma, is would be easy to focus upon the physical products of her activities and suggest that she made a puppet and theatre and that this was therefore essentially a 'Design and Technology' activity. This is disingenuous as Jemma did not set out with an explicit plan for these physical outcomes or ever indicate that these were important to her. She demonstrated many aspects of learning including interpretation of character, responding to music, creative role-play, shape and space, fine motor skills, negotiation, critical thinking, independence, imagination, problem-solving, and team work. As practitioners we can observe for involvement by looking for more than single-minded perseverance towards a planned goal, typified by the 'what is it?' question about a child's picture or model, towards an attention to process. Laevers (2005b) argues that it is the process of learning that should be our focus as educators, as the real outcomes of learning are much longer term. Similarly, it is the process of levelling involvement and well-being, the sustained noticing and analysis and subsequent shared dialogue, that is important in using levels of involvement in practice rather than the levels themselves.

Nurturing involvement through assessment

In its simplest form feelings of involvement are nurtured where you feel you are known and valued. Assessment, particularly observation, therefore has a crucial role to play in nurturing involvement with types, timing and interpretation of observations being essential elements. As practitioners we try to ensure that we undertake detailed observations of children's significant moments in learning (Smidt, 2009) and that this guides observation timing rather than observation schedules and routines. Carr (2001: 5) notes optimally that: 'Attention has shifted from internal structures and representations in the mind to meaning-making, intention, and relationships in the experienced world' and offers, through 'learning stories', a credit- rather than deficit-based assessment.

This enables us to build upon moments of deep learning where children have experienced their highest levels of involvement and we view children as competent learners (Fisher, 2013). This continues to challenge us as practitioners, particularly within mixed-age settings where diverse levels of involvement overlap within a busy setting, particularly where physical space is limited.

Observation supports practitioners in identifying where children feel that their high involvement activities are at risk. The evidence of potential threats and barriers to involvement is there for us to see if we utilise observation effectively. We can sometimes, for example, see children literally fencing off their play and activity and creating barriers and markers, signalling with clear intention that this is 'my space to play'. Tuning into children through observation enables us to see these clearly communicated signals and adapt our provision to nurture children's involvement through providing opportunities to engage with possibilities in learning in this sustained and deeper way. Open observation, without narrow purpose or agenda and attention to involvement, supports us to really *see* the child and ensure that evidence collected is authentic. Well-being and involvement are indicative of the effectiveness of the holistic learning environment. This is powerful in terms of supporting the development of provision and practice. It allows us to take responsibility for children's learning without taking control of it.

The Leuven Involvement Scale supports us in identifying higher and lower levels of involvement within the diverse range of observed experiences that occur across an enormous variety of settings. As Woods points out in Chapter 2, these scales are accessible, simple and produce broad agreement, which is perhaps indicative of why they have had such a wide and sustained impact. These are readily communicable and so provide us with a tool and language through which we can engage in meaningful dialogue about a child's learning. The purpose and intent of observing well-being and involvement resonate with early years practitioners as they attend to fundamentals that we hold as central to our values as educators: children's happiness and learning. Bourdieu (1998: 2) states that: 'The deepest logic of the social world can be grasped only if one plunges into the particularity of an empirical reality, historically located and dated.'

This approach is ultimately valuing of the child, as it does not assume to know them or to live in their world. Through observation we seek to uncover insights into the child's world whilst acknowledging that we are tourists and interpreters within childhood, which links to James *et al.*'s (1998) notion of children being a distinct tribe. In this way observation supports us in bridging the adult and child worlds and provides access for practitioners to see into the child's experience. We seek to find out what it is like to be *this* child in *this* educational setting at this moment in time. We observe the child's lived experience of learning, documenting 'what it means to a young child to live and take part in the educational setting' (Laevers and Heylen, 2003: 13). This lived experience is the 'layered emotions, action and conceptions' (Løndal, 2010: 393), which is only truly enabled by actual experience (Merleau-Ponty, 2005).

Assessing through observation, recorded and momentary, assumes that each child will not behave in the same way as any other. This challenges our sometimes natural inclinations as practitioners, particularly experienced practitioners, to spot patterns, label and group children in our perceptions so as to 'see' one child as similar to one we worked with a few years ago, typically predetermined to be a certain way or to fit within a checklist of attributes. Observation using levels of involvement enables us to truly assess each child as a unique individual, in a way that many assessments do not, whilst providing evidence that can contribute in a meaningful way towards comparative or criterion driven assessments and can also support quality development of provision.

The relationship between observer and child is an important factor in successful observation of involvement, as different children are involved in different ways and therefore involvement presents itself differently. Knowledge of the child is therefore crucial. This is illustrated by an encounter with Kyra who complains that a child has knocked over 'the first aid elephant'. Knowledge of Kyra's world means knowing that she attends a primary school nursery as well as a day care nursery and that her play may be representative of her experiences in these different contexts.

Encounter: Kyra and the first aid elephant

Kyra is lying on the floor lining up toy animals in rows with several animals nearest Kyra seemingly yet to be placed in rows. The practitioner watches Kyra and considers her to be engaged in purposeful activity with moderate levels of involvement. She seems to be placing the animals in approximately uniform rows but without sorting or purpose to the placing; her gaze remains on the animals throughout but she remains lying on the floor moving only her arms and occasionally resting her head on her arm. Lucas rushes past with a paper aeroplane and runs through the animals knocking over one of them. Kyra sits up immediately and scans the animals, frowning and declaring loudly, 'Hey!' and complains to the practitioner, 'Lucas knocked over the first aid elephant!' Through dialogue between Kyra and the practitioner, Kyra enthusiastically reveals that the small world animals are teachers and pupils in a school. The animals at the front are carefully selected to be the head teacher and two 'visitors' in assembly and the elephant at the back is the teaching assistant who is performing first aid on one of the 'children' (the hippopotamus) who hurt themselves at playtime. The animals at the end of each row are the school staff next to their classes.

In this encounter, knowledge of the multiple learning contexts of the child is essential to understanding her higher levels of involvement than might have first appeared by watching her place small world animals in lines. She is much more mentally active than the practitioner had at first thought. Tuning into the language ('first aid'), knowledge of the child and engaging in conversation supported the practitioner in accurately assessing Kyra's level of involvement in this activity. This included the level of satisfaction evident in her enthusiastic sharing of her thinking and her defensive dissatisfaction when she felt Lucas posed a threat to her work. The accurate assessment of involvement through observation is essential in planning appropriate activities and adaptations to the environment in order to develop and sustain high levels of involvement and therefore deep learning. Here, we need to acknowledge both a pedagogical and ethical commitment to dispositional learning and assessment and recognise that the daily routines and activities will reflect the way we plan and assess. Woods and Wardle (2013: 111) cite Siraj-Blatchford and Manni (2007: 28); see also McEwan's and Kent's chapters in this volume.

The steps you as a leader can take include demonstrating the skills to:

- identify and articulate collective vision, especially with regard to pedagogy and curriculum;
- ensure shared understandings, meanings and goals;
- communicate effectively;
- encourage reflection;
- monitor and assess practice;
- show a commitment to ongoing, professional development;
- build a learning community and team culture;
- encourage parent and community partnerships.

Nurturing involvement through planning

Planning as an 'active process which helps us look ahead' (Bruce *et al.*, 2015: xv) enacts our interpretation of the knowledge we have gained through assessment. This can be 'in the moment', as well as for sessions, weeks or longer time periods. This direct correlation between assessment and planning means that whatever we attend to within assessment is what we also attend to in our planning and practice. Through planning informed by observation-based assessment, practitioners can nurture children's involvement and plan provision to include possibilities that reflect what or how they have shown interest and also what they might find interesting but have not yet encountered. Taking this approach we plan to increase the possibilities in learning for the child and support them in getting deeply involved within one or more of them. As practitioners we are then planning for the learner they are now as well as the learner they might become. We recognise the 'developing child' and do not limit the child to learning within their previous capabilities, opportunities or experiences (Laevers and Verboven, 2000). Within a symbiotic relationship, the effects of the child upon their activity and the activity upon the child, high levels of involvement are characterised by the two when they become indistinguishably fused as one. Laevers (2006) refers to the notion of this being seamless with no distance between child and activity. Removing all that might create distance between child and activity and therefore is an important purpose of our planning.

In planning to nurture children's involvement, we can plan rich, diverse and interesting contexts that contain many opportunities to find fascination, so that the child can focus on this fascination and learn deeply (Bruce, 2012). Such fascination is illustrated by an encounter with Max who is 18 months old.

Encounter: Max and the fish tank

Despite many books, toys and ride-on vehicles (which are a particular favourite of his) in the room, he watches the fish tank with its two very small fish with fascination. Attempts to coax him away include a biscuit, a ball and a car but he still remains at the fish tank. He makes noises as the fish moves and turns his head and crouches down to see from different angles. As the fish swims through a rock with a hole in it, his whole body shivers with excitement.

In planning to nurture involvement, the child is at the centre of the process. They have ownership of their learning and are trusted to learn, being viewed as being good at learning. As our earlier consideration of the encounter with Jemma suggests, children need to have ownership of learning goals, which do not need to relate to tangible products, and be able to change these frequently within activities. As Woods explains in Chapter 1, even within adult-led activity the child with high levels of involvement has redesigned and reimagined the activity for themselves; the goal or objective is therefore ultimately the child's.

In planning, we need to support involvement in a genuine way. To follow a child's interests is to be guided by the child. We therefore need to plan explicitly for this through ensuring that staff roles, timetables and resources enable adults to be guided by children within a secure familiar environment where children feel able to lead. With the best intentions, there are very real dangers in using interests to 'sell' learning to children or coerce children to be enthusiastic through planning for stimuli to act as 'hooks' for learning or enticements; for example, a set of flashcards are no more following a child's interests if they are branded with a children's television character; the 'interests' in this respect are clearly the adult ones. Within this we consider how they learn as well as where and what they learn. These 'interests' need to be authentic and contextualised. The fundamental question for us as practitioners is, 'where and when have they experienced higher levels of involvement?' rather than, 'what are the child's interests?' as it is the former that will enable us to nurture involvement through our planning. Similarly, issues can also exist where children are invited to care about education within the adult realm; for example, to get a 'good' job, to make an adult happy, fear or reprisals, or because they will be tested on it later. Anxiety-induced engagement is not engagement at all but a hyper-presence within which learning is inhibited and negative perceptions of education can manifest.

Children following their own ideas and making choices for themselves within the endless possibilities afforded within the setting nurtures feelings of ownership and support involvement.

> Planning for possibilities rather than outcomes switches the dynamics of planning. Here, the practitioner's role is to facilitate learning, to follow rather than lead. The control and responsibility is more balanced in its distribution, thus resting much more with the child. The plans are determined by an 'insider', the child, supported and enabled by the practitioner.
>
> (Gripton, 2013: 8)

Higher levels of involvement are evident where children feel that they have responsibility and where therefore anything is possible. This is supported by emotional connections with activities that are meaningful for the individual child. In this way we cannot plan *for children* but plan *for children to plan*; our role is to provide possibility rich contexts. Perceptions of choice are significant within this as a child only has genuine choice where they are fully aware of the choices they have and enact these. A child who repeatedly revisits the same activity might be choosing to do this or could be less autonomous, or feel that this activity is where the adult wants them to go. Similarly a child visiting a range of activities could be following another child or an adult without feeling they can choose an alternative. Donaldson (1978: 94) is persuasive: 'We heighten our awareness of what is actual by consideration of what is possible.'

Emotional investment is fundamental within involvement. This relates to risk-taking and the need for an environment that supports children to feel able to make outward emotional commitments and risk sharing of themselves. As Brown explains in depth in Chapter 3, the physical learning environment is a crucial aspect of our planning for possibilities. This is not a busy, packed or brightly coloured environment but one where simple resources are organised in ways that support children in making connections and provide spaces for them to engage with these. Through it, we support children to engage with possibilities and can nurture their involvement to facilitate deep and significant development in learning. The physical environment can be organised so as to reduce the potential for children to feel overwhelmed or confused by the variety, busyness and scale within their setting. As we embrace the notion of infinite possibilities for children's learning, we recognise that when experiencing high levels of involvement, children rarely connect with a great number of possibilities simultaneously. Involvement requires opportunities to engage with a range of possibilities with the time and permission to follow one of these possibilities and become highly invested within it. This is supported by children's extended and continuous access, freedom, responsibility and trust with physical spaces and resources, as well as with practitioners and other children. As described by Gripton (2013), planning for endless possibilities includes truly open-ended resources, a timetable that provides more extended periods of child-initiated play, and the provision of spaces and systems to enable activity to continue across breaks within the timetable, including between sessions.

The role of the adult is crucial, as McEwan describes in Chapter 5, because children's successful outcomes are determined by the pedagogical relationships and practices of educators (Laevers and Heylen, 2003). As practitioners, we can utilise language effectively within interactions with children to support them in seeing future possibilities as an integral part of their present so that their approach to their surroundings becomes more independent of the concrete (Vygotsky, 1978). We can also plan to encourage a curious 'eagerness for experience' (Dewey, 1910: 30) or 'exploratory need' (Laevers, 1998: 84) through providing resources and contexts that are rich in opportunities to find wonder and therefore align with children's innate desire to learn (Donaldson, 1978). Practitioners are key in supporting social aspects of learning, providing social stimuli within activities, spaces and adult-led provision. Modelling is also crucial. Adults should model habits of curiosity and involvement; modelling how continuity of thought requires flexibility of activity (Dewey, 1910). They should themselves be highly involved (Laevers, 2006).

It is essential for children that practitioners recognise lower levels of involvement and support children through nurturing deeper engagement with possibilities. Lower levels of involvement can be often misunderstood, particularly with younger children or where behaviour is deemed 'disruptive'. Bourdieu (1998) points out that investment arises from an invested relationship with the context; therefore 'disruptive' behaviour such as fighting over a toy suggests a level of involvement with their activity and the setting more generally. Our response needs to be one of taking responsibility. This requires us to model, observe, show faith in the child, take a 'can do' approach, be valuing of the child and have a growth mindset (Dweck, 2008). We can actively seek out barriers to learning and take measures to ameliorate them, drawing upon our openness and willingness to change our practice and our setting. Where low levels of involvement are apparent, barriers to involvement can be addressed instead of enticements provided. Whole child support can be provided, instead of specific remedial action, and a personalised and nurturing curriculum may be planned, supported by gentle measures to nurture self-esteem and confidence. For these and all children, we can consider possibilities for involvement. Within the understanding that we all have a range of levels of involvement every day, we can plan for activities to vary in length, be collaborative or individual, and feel familiar or new, to provide scope for involvement across the child's experiences within the setting. Sharing observation evidence such as photographs and learning stories, we can reflect together with children upon when they are most involved, to help us to understand them as a learner and see this within them.

Conclusion

Involvement breeds involvement. Working within a culture of involvement, children *and adults* find interest and fascination in the interest of others. This can occur in a multitude of ways including through their body language, facial expression, manipulation and presentation of objects, through dialogue and sustained shared thinking. Within an environment of involvement, individual and groups of children are immersed within following different possibilities. Within this type of environment children who are involved for shorter periods or are less involved are quicker to become involved and re-engaged owing to the range of opportunities for involvement afforded to them and the focused environment. In the spirit of Crowe's (1983) 'play is a feeling', involvement is a feeling and an atmosphere as well as an observable engagement of a child within activity. There is something mesmeric and magical about a child absorbed within an activity or idea; watching it is one of the greatest privileges of working with children and feeling it is one of the greatest pleasures of being a child.

Provocations

- When do you regard a child's activity to be finished? Is it when the child chooses to leave it? When the child achieves balance and feels satisfied? When there is a tangible product? When it begins to appear disorganised? When it is 'tidy up' time?
- How do you see a 'flow' of involvement in children's play? What type of situations and contexts seem to support, encourage and nurture flow?
- When observing levels of involvement do you perceive involvement with a singular activity as being at a higher level than with several activities? Do you perceive higher levels of involvement within particular activities that you deem more challenging to maintain engagement with?
- How are your perceptions of involvement communicated to children? Do you expect or praise higher levels of involvement within specific circumstances? Are lower levels of involvement sometimes rewarded if they seem less disruptive, quiet, orderly or easier to manage?
- Do you talk to children when observing them or following observation of them? Does this provide further information about their involvement, purposes and choices? Could you use conversation to a greater extent to support observation and therefore your understanding of the child's involvement?
- Is there a recognition within your setting that levels of involvement are naturally fluid for all children and that every child (and adult) needs to experience this flux within every day?

- How could planning and assessment processes within your setting be adapted or enhanced by greater attention to levels of involvement?
- Do you model (including verbalising) flexibility within sustained involvement? Do children see you deepening your engagement through changing activity, adapting resources and varying your purposes?
- Do you allow time for transitions within involvement where a child is moving between trains of thought, lines of possibilities or purposes and might still return back previous activity, adapt the activity or move away from it completely?
- To what extent do you see evidence of the children feeling and enacting the choices they have within your setting?

References

Bourdieu, P. (1998) *Practical Reason. On the Theory of Action*. Oxford: Polity.

Bruce, T. (2012) *Early Childhood Practice. Froebel Today*. London: Sage.

Bruce, T., Louis, S. and McCall, G. (2015) *Observing Young Children*. London: Sage.

Carr, M. (2001) *Assessment in Early Childhood Settings. Learning Stories*. London: PCP.

Craft, A. (2002) *Creativity and Early Years Education. A Lifewide Foundation*. London: Continuum.

Crowe, B. (1983) *Play is a Feeling*. London: Allen & Unwin.

Csíkszentmihályi, M. (2002) *Flow. The Classic Work on How to Achieve Happiness*. 2nd edn. London: Rider.

Dewey, J. (1910) *How We Think*. Boston: D. C. Heath & Co.

Donaldson, M. (1978) *Children's Minds*. London: Croom Helm.

Dweck, C. S. (2008) *Mindset. The New Psychology of Success*. New York: Ballantine Books.

Fisher, J. (2013) *Starting from the Child. Teaching and Learning in the Foundation Stage*. Maidenhead: McGraw-Hill International.

Gripton, C. (2013) Planning for endless possibilities. In Woods, A. (ed.) *Child-initiated Play and Learning. Planning for Possibilities in the Early Years*. London: David Fulton, pp. 8–21.

James, A., Jenks, C. and Prout, A. (1998) *Theorizing Childhood*. Cambridge: Polity Press.

Laevers, F. (ed.) (1994) *The Leuven Involvement Scale for Young Children, LIS-YC*. Manual. Leuven, Belgium: Centre for Experiential Education.

Laevers, F. (1998) Understanding the world of objects and of people. Intuition as the core element of deep level learning. *International Journal of Educational Research*, 29(1): 69–86.

Laevers, F. (2000) Forward to basics! Deep-level learning and the experiential approach. *Early Years*, 20(2): 20–29.

Laevers, F. (2002) Forward to basics! Deep-level-learning and the experiential approach. *Indivisa: Boletin de Estudios e Investigación*, 3: 9–18.

Laevers, F. (2005a). The curriculum as means to raise the quality of early childhood education. Implications for policy. *European Early Childhood Education Research Journal*, 13(1): 17–29.

Laevers, F. (2005b) *Deep-level Learning and the Experiential Approach in Early Childhood and Primary Education*. Belgium: Katholieke Universiteit Leuven, Research Centre for Early Childhood and Primary Education.

Laevers, F. (2006) *A Process-oriented Child Monitoring System for Young Children*. Leuven, Belgium: CEGO Publishers.

Laevers, F. and Heylen, L. (eds) (2003) *Involvement of Children and Teacher Style. Insights from an International Study on Experiential Education. Studia Paedagogica 35*. Leuven, Belgium: Leuven University Press.

Laevers, F. and Verboven, L. (2000) Gender related role patterns in preschool settings. Can 'experiential education' make a difference? *European Early Childhood Education Research Journal*, 8(1): 25–42.

Løndal, K. (2010) Children's lived experience and their sense of coherence. Bodily play in a Norwegian after-school programme. *Child Care in Practice*, 16(4): 391–407.

Merleau-Ponty, M. (2005) *Phenomenology of Perception*. London: Taylor & Francis.

Smidt, S. (2009) *Planning for the Early Years Foundation Stage*. London: Routledge.

Vygotsky, L. S. (1978) *Mind in Society: The Development of Higher Psychological Processes*. London: Harvard University Press.

Woods, A. (ed.) (2013) *Child-initiated Play and Learning. Planning for Possibilities in the Early Years*. London: David Fulton.

Woods, A. and Wardle, L. (2013) Leading possibilities. In Woods, A. (ed.) *Child-initiated Play and Learning: Planning for Possibilities in the Early Years*. London: Routledge, Chapter 8.

Index